SUPERNATURAL
MID-ATLANTIC

Laurie Hull

Schiffer Publishing Ltd

4880 Lower Valley Road • Atglen, PA 19310

DEDICATION

TO THE SPIRITS THAT WALK AMONG US,
MAY THEY FIND PEACE.

Ouija® is a registered trademark of Parker Brothers Games
Raystown Ray™ is a registered trademark by Wilderness Editions
Text and images by author unless otherwise noted

Schiffer Books are available at special discounts for bulk purchases for sales promotions or premiums. Special editions, including personalized covers, corporate imprints, and excerpts can be created in large quantities for special needs. For more information contact the publisher:

Published by Schiffer Publishing, Ltd.
4880 Lower Valley Road
Atglen, Pennsylvania 19310
Phone: (610) 593-1777; Fax: (610) 593-2002
E-mail: Info@schifferbooks.com

For the largest selection of fine reference books on this and related subjects,
please visit our website at **www.schifferbooks.com**
We are always looking for people to write books on new and related subjects.
If you have an idea for a book, please contact us at
proposals@schifferbooks.com

This book may be purchased from the publisher.
Please try your bookstore first.
You may write for a free catalog.

In Europe, Schiffer books are distributed by
Bushwood Books
6 Marksbury Ave.
Kew Gardens
Surrey TW9 4JF England
Phone: 44 (0) 20 8392 8585; Fax: 44 (0) 20 8392 9876
E-mail: info@bushwoodbooks.co.uk
Website: www.bushwoodbooks.co.uk

Other Schiffer Books By The Author:

Brandywine Valley Ghosts   978-0-7643-3041-4 $12.99
Philly's Main Line Haunts   978-0-7643-3181-7 $14.99
Supernatural Pennsylvania   978-0-7643-3606-5 $24.99
Cape May Haunts: Elaine's Haunted Mansion and Other Eerie Beach Tales (with D. P. Roseberry)
978-0-7643-2821-3 $14.95

Designed by Mark David Bowyer
Type set in AlgerianBasD / Zurich BT

ISBN: 978-0-7643-4119-9
Printed in the United States of America

CONTENTS

CONTENTS

Historic Buildings:

Schools and Universities:

Hotels and Restaurants:

Battlefields and Forts:

BURIED TREASURE AND PIRATE GHOSTS

CONCLUSION

APPENDIX

ACKNOWLEDGMENTS

This book would not have been written were it not for the support and encouragement of my family, especially my husband, Pauric. I want to thank my family for being patient with and understanding my obsession with the supernatural, and for visiting countless haunted places with me. In addition to my family, I am also grateful to Bill Horton, Lori Clark, Fred DiCostanzo, Mike Meehan, and Rich Hickman for sharing their stories and photos. Without them, investigating the paranormal would not be the same and I know Tri County Paranormal couldn't exist without them.

Big thanks also to Dinah, my editor, for her patience and understanding and for continuing to be an inspiration to me.

*The most beautiful
thing we can
experience is the
mysterious. It is the
source of all true art
and science*.

~Albert Einstein

INTRODUCTION

It is hard to resist going out to investigate reports of miracles, apparitions, and what are known as "thin places," places where the veil that separates the physical from the spirit world is at its thinnest. I have always been fascinated by anything supernatural. Whether it is ghosts, psychics, miracles, or anything else slightly resembling something supernatural, you can bet I'll be trying to learn all I can about it. My interest in the supernatural began at an early age, when I lived in a very haunted house where I was reminded daily that we share this world with spirits.

I think that is all it takes to get started—one brush with something unexplained, something supernatural, that gets us seekers going and keeps us going. We continue to research stories, hunt down leads, and search for explanations for the unexplained that continually elude us.

My own house was the first in a long line of haunted places I have investigated. It remains, to this day, the most frightening place I have ever been in. During my efforts to understand what was going on there, I had talked to many people about the occurrences at my house. Before long, people began to tell me about local haunted places and of their experiences with the supernatural.

I have had the good fortune to have lived in Pennsylvania, New Jersey, and Virginia, and experienced paranormal events at all of these places. Sometimes I think it follows me around; other times I think I find it because I am looking for it.

The Mid-Atlantic is, in my opinion, one of the supernatural hotspots of the world. With so much history, it is almost expected that we would have ghosts here, left over from those battles for independence and more battles to keep it. Just the sheer volume of people who have lived and died here is bound to give rise to a lingering lovelorn lady, a pirate guarding his treasure, or a Native American protecting his sacred ground. During the writing of this book, I came to the realization that the supernatural is all around us; it can happen at any time, to anyone, especially in the Mid-Atlantic. Just a drive to a local shop can include a haunted cemetery among the scenery. In an hour's drive between any two points, one can have countless brushes with the otherworldly, even in the most ordinary-looking places, and especially in the places featured in this book.

MYSTICAL POWER PLACES

Don't have to travel to Macchu Picchu, Stonehenge, or Lourdes to experience the power of a mystical place, especially when the Mid-Atlantic region has so many. Rosicrucians, Sacred Stones, and Miraculous Sites are all within a day's drive of each other.

CAVES

Caves are holes in the earth that may occur naturally or may have been dug out by humans. Caves have been used by humans for many purposes since prehistoric times, including housing and ceremonial uses. Since it is a space inside the earth, the caves are sometimes thought of as the womb of Mother Earth and are associated with female energies of rebirth and regeneration.

CAVE OF KELPIUS
PENNSYLVANIA

If you are on Hermit Lane, you are nearly there. Some claim that this is an old springhouse and it may have been used for storage during part of its history, but there is no denying the energy there. A marker placed there by the Rosicrucian Brotherhood states that this place was where Rosicrucian master Johannes Kelpius came for shelter and to meditate. Rosicrucians are a secret society dedicated to teaching and practicing ancient spiritual traditions and knowledge in order to better understand nature, the universe, and the spiritual world.

Johannes Kelpius and his group arrived in the late seventeenth century and were sought out by locals for their knowledge of healing and astronomy. The order called themselves The Society of the Woman in the Wilderness, which may have been a reference to the Magdalene mysteries and the Holy Grail. It is said that the order disbanded when Kelpius died in the early 1700s. Others say that Kelpius didn't die because he had found the secret of immortality.

Some descriptions of Kelpius and his group say that they came to the Wissahickon to watch the end of the world. This is likely a misconception; as Rosicrucians, they would be focused on bringing about a shift in consciousness to a higher level for all humans – a new world in the New World. As they lived in what was then wilderness, they did witness the end of the Old World, as the New World in North America was being born. Mystics like Rosicrucians rarely communicate in a straightforward way, so this philosophy of the death of the old way was likely misinterpreted to mean they were looking for a literal end of the world.

Why were Kelpius and his followers drawn to this spot? The Wissahickon area has some of the oldest exposed rock in North America. If those rocks could talk, they may have spoken to him and his followers, urging them to walk in the footsteps of many who had passed before. The place is not easy to find, but worth the hike. The feeling of timelessness as one enters the area is indescribable.

The Cave of Kelpius overlooks the Wissahickon.
Photo Courtesy of Rich Hickman.

TRAVELER'S NOTE

Located above the Wissahickon Creek near Hermit Lane.

INDIAN ECHO CAVERNS
PENNSYLVANIA

Indian Echo Caverns was first used by the Susquehannock Indians who lived and hunted in the area. It is said that the Susquehannock used the Indian Ballroom for initiation ceremonies, but they avoided the Rainbow Room, which they felt was home to evil spirits. According to D.W. Hauck's book, *Haunted Places*, many visitors have seen the angry ghost of a Native American man holding the severed head of a bearded white man in the Rainbow Room. Possibly this is a residual kind of warning for people to keep out of this area.

A HERMIT'S HOME

The cave has been visited by the White Man since 1783; most notably it became the home of hermit William Wilson, who retreated after he arrived too late with a pardon for his sister, Elizabeth, who had just been executed in Chester, Pennsylvania. Elizabeth had been found guilty of murdering her twin children whom had been born out of wedlock in 1784. He was so devastated by the loss that he wandered west from Chester and ended up living in this cave until his death in 1821.

The cave was also the home of the Mystery Box, which was found in there in the early 1900s by some local boys who were exploring the cave. In the 1960s, one of the boys returned the box and its contents, which were a collection of very old coins and instructions on making diamonds out of coal.

TRAVELER'S NOTE

368 Middletown Road,
Hummelstown, Pennsylvania 17036
www.indianechocaverns.com/

SACRED STONES

Stones and rock formations have been invested with mysterious powers for thousands of years. "In olden times all the Greeks worshipped unwrought stones instead of images."[1]

As early as 5000 BC, megaliths, or large stones, were set up across Europe in lines and circles, such as Stonehenge in England. Not much is known about these stone circles, but it is generally agreed they were placed for some sacred purpose.

Not all sacred stones are megalithic structures; some small and individual stones have been invested with great power as well. One example of this is the single Stone of Destiny at the Hill of Tara in Ireland, which was used in coronation ceremonies of ancient Kings of Ireland.

The Stone of Destiny at the Hill of Tara.

TRIPOD ROCK
NEW JERSEY

This interesting rock formation, which scientists say was left when the glaciers receded after the Ice Age, has spoken to those who will listen for centuries. It was said by the less scientific to have been levitated into its present position by a powerful Native American shaman.

The truly remarkable part is that on the summer solstice (June 21st) the sun sets between the marker rocks here. This produces an amazing sense of peace and power in viewers.

There are actually three tripod rocks on the mountain. The park rangers credit a glacier with the making of Tripod Rock, and human hands with the creation of the Solstice Rocks. The theory is that the solstice rocks were placed by Native Americans to mark a ceremonial site.

TRAVELER'S NOTE

Pyramid Mountain County Park
Kinnelon, New Jersey
www.morrisparks.net/aspparks/pyrmtnmain.asp

RINGING ROCKS
PENNSYLVANIA

Bring a small hammer when you visit Ringing Rocks Park in Bucks County, Pennsylvania. If you hit the rocks in the field of boulders with the hammer or another rock, they make a ringing sound similar to banging on a pipe. There are lots of interesting theories about how the rocks got there and why they ring, but none have been proven. Everything from a rapid freeze-thaw cycle to extra terrestrial origin has been put forward as an explanation for the unusual ringing property of the rocks.

TRAVELER'S NOTE

Ringing Rocks Road
Upper Black Eddy, Pennsylvania 18972
www.buckscounty.org/government/departments/parksandrec/parks/
ringingrocks.aspx

OLEY HILLS
PENNSYLVANIA

Located in Berks County, Pennsylvania, is an interesting complex of stone cairns, stone rows, platforms, and terraces. Some believe the structures to be colonial in origin and others believe they are Native American. It is possible they are a mixture of both, with the colonists making use of existing stone structures and even expanding them to their uses.

The most fascinating section consists of a stone structure with a flat roof. At its north end, a series of terraces extends toward some large boulders. This area gives the impression of having been the center of something, or the focal point, but it is not clear what its original purpose or use may have been.

The feeling on visiting these complexes is one of awe and wonder. Although some of the arrangements may be attributed to glacial movement, there is no doubt that human hands constructed the terraces and structures. It is even possible to discern animal and human forms in some of the rock piles and boulders, but whether those images were made intentionally by the builders or are a result of the imaginations of the observers has not been determined.

In addition to these, Oley Hills also contains a huge split boulder with another stone wedged into the split. The whole thing is abandoned now and an expectant hush lies over the area, almost as if the structures are awaiting the return of someone.

TRAVELER'S NOTE

Berks County, Pennsylvania

LOST VALLEY ROCKS
PENNSYLVANIA

A man named Gary Yannone believes that the natural springs on his property were a focal point of a ceremonial site of a prehistoric culture. He has found many rocks that seem to be carved into human faces or shaped into various animals, such as wolves.

Some scientists who have visited the property to see the rocks have stated that the rocks are older than other Iroquois, Susquehannock, and Delaware artifacts that have been found in the area. Other scientists do not believe the rocks are evidence of a prehistoric culture, but believers are not swayed by this skepticism. They have compared the rock images to those found in cave paintings in France and other parts of Europe. The animal rocks may have been left there as offerings for whatever god or goddess was believed to inhabit the springs.

Perhaps as more artifacts are unearthed the truth will be uncovered as well and we will know for sure whether this was an ancient sacred site.

TRAVELER'S NOTE

Lower Frankford Township, Cumberland Valley, Pennsylvania

BALD FRIAR ROCKS
MARYLAND

Petroglyphs, or rock carvings, are found throughout the Mid-Atlantic region. They are important in helping us to get a glimpse of the cultures that existed here when the European settlers arrived on the scene. Some of the glyphs are trail markers; others mark tribal territories or important spiritual places. Some of them even tell stories. Not all glyphs are easily understood by us, as many of them are thousands of years old and the exact meanings of the symbols have been lost or obscured through translation by other cultures. Although the exact site of the Bald Friar Petro glyphs is now underwater, the carvings were preserved in pieces and currently reside at the Historical Societies of Cecil and Harford Counties, Maryland, and some are also held at the Maryland Historical Trust's Archaeological Conservation Lab.

What makes the Bald Friar petroglyphs unique is the prominence of a serpent's head motif which does not appear in other petroglyph sites. This could represent a different tribal area, but it is very close to another site twenty miles away which does not contain the symbol. The meaning of this glyph remains a mystery, but one thing is certain. When viewing the glyphs, one cannot help but feel the deep spiritual meaning that the symbol seems to convey, very much like our archetypal symbols speak to us.

TRAVELER'S NOTE

The rescued petroglyphs are now at three locations: (1) outside the Harford County Courthouse in Bel Air, (2) at the Cecil County Public Library in Elkton, and (3) Druid Hill Park in Baltimore.

RELIGIOUS SHRINES

A shrine is a holy or sacred place, dedicated to a certain deity, saint, or hero. They usually contain some type of relic or object that is associated with the being the shrine is for and are found in most of the religions of the world, including Christianity, Hinduism, Buddhism, and Wicca.

SHRINE OF ST. JOHN NEUMANN
PENNSYLVANIA

John Neumann was the first American man to be canonized. The shrine contains the actual body of St. John Neumann, enclosed in a glass case under the main altar. Several miraculous healings have been attributed to St. John Neumann, including one of a man who was crushed between a car and a utility pole and a child who was diagnosed with Ewing's Sarcoma and was given six months to live. The cures were considered to be scientifically and medically inexplicable and were called miraculous.

In addition to healing miracles, the body of the saint has remained undecayed or incorrupt and when there was a fire in the church where the body lies, nearby items were reduced to ash, but St. John Neumann was not effected in any way. Even the wax mask over his face was not melted!

TRAVELER'S NOTE

1019 North Fifth Street
Philadelphia, Pennsylvania 19123
www.stjohnneumann.org/

SHRINE OF ST. KATHARINE DREXEL
PENNSYLVANIA

Katharine Drexel was born into a very wealthy family, and she dedicated her life and inheritance to the needs of oppressed Native Americans and African-Americans in the western and southwestern United States. To address racial injustice and destitution and spread the Gospel to these groups, she established a religious order, the Sisters of the Blessed Sacrament for Indians and Colored People. She also financed more than sixty missions and schools around the United States; in addition, she founded Xavier University of Louisiana, which is the only historically Black, Catholic university in the U.S.

People who visit the burial site of Saint Katharine Drexel place their needs and requests in an open prayer basket. She has been credited with causing deaf people to be able to hear.

St. Katharine Drexel's tomb.

TRAVELER'S NOTE

1663 Bristol Pike
Bensalem, Pennsylvania 19020
www.katharinedrexel.org/

SHRINE OF ST. ELIZABETH SETON
MARYLAND

St. Elizabeth Seton was the first saint born in America and is the patron saint of the United States. The shrine, located in Emmitsburg, Maryland, is an easy drive from Gettysburg, Pennsylvania. Elizabeth Seton was a wife, mother, widow, sole parent, foundress, educator, minister, and spiritual leader. She decided to convert to Catholicism during a visit to Italy that was undertaken to try to restore her husband's bad health. She lost two of her children to tuberculosis. The trip to Italy did not save her husband. He died there in Pisa. Elizabeth returned to the United States without her husband, but with a burning faith in Roman Catholicism that led her to found the religious order of the Sisters of Charity in the United States.

Sadly, Elizabeth herself succumbed to tuberculosis, but her strong faith in the face of adversity was an inspiration for many and the mission she started continues today. People travel from all over to visit the shrine and pray for the intercession of St. Elizabeth Seton. She has been credited with miraculous healings of rare forms of cancer and encephalitis.

The Shrine of St. Elizabeth Seton.

TRAVELER'S NOTE

333 South Seton Avenue
Emmitsburg, Maryland 21727
www.setonshrine.org/

FOUNTAIN OF YOUTH
DELAWARE

This is a well built over a spring that has been known for about 300 years now as possessing supernatural properties. Although no one has yet come forward to claim that the waters of this spring have restored or preserved their youth, the legend remains that those who drink from the well will have their youth preserved or restored.

TRAVELER'S NOTE

The fountain is now on private property and cannot be visited, but the idea that it is still there is fascinating.

UNEXPLAINED CREATURES

Creatures whose existence has been believed but not proven by current science are known as a cryptids. The most famous cryptids are probably Bigfoot and the Loch Ness Monster. Proof of their existence is usually limited to anecdotal evidence.

RAYSTOWN RAY
PENNSYLVANIA

Raystown Lake is a man-made lake that was created in the early part of the twentieth century. At that time, it was a shallow lake. The lake was enlarged and deepened in 1973 to provide a recreational lake and resort. So how did a creature like Raystown Ray end up in a man-made lake?

HOAX?

It may be a hoax, some say, created to get people to come to the lake. Look what Nessie did for Loch Ness! The sheer volume of sightings of Raystown Ray is compelling. It is said to look similar to the Loch Ness Monster. Different people seeing the same creature at different times point to something being there. Either this is a very well-thought out marketing plan or there really *is* something in that man-made lake.

An interesting tidbit that I found was that when the plans were made to deepen the lake: Teams from Juniata College and Penn State University excavated a stone-age shelter called Sheep Rock Shelter. Human remains dated at 6,000 years old were recovered from the site and removed to a museum. Is it possible that the disruption of this sacred site unleashed a curse on the lake or did the dig open up something else; a possible connection between this world and another, where monsters exist?

TRAVELER'S NOTE

Raystown, Pennsylvania
Firsthand accounts of sightings are collected at www.raystownray.com.

BIGFOOT

The Mid-Atlantic has its very own Bigfoot reports and agencies that take reports of sightings.

PENNSYLVANIA

There is the Pennsylvania Bigfoot Society at www.pabigfootsociety. com, and Stan Gordon at www.stangordonufo.com. Both sites list report after report of eight-to-nine-foot hair-covered creatures that smell like rotten eggs. They have photos of footprints left by these creatures, some of which measure eighteen inches! It is theorized that these creatures are living in the network of abandoned mines scattered around the state of Pennsylvania.

NEW JERSEY

According to www.njbigfoot.org:

Witness reports...detail encounters with large, hairy monsters in the wilderness of Northern New Jersey and areas south, even at the

Jersey shore. Bigfoot has been seen in West Milford, Sussex, High Point, Wantage, Walpack, Landing, Stillwater, New Gretna…and other locations around New Jersey.[2]

The site lists report after report of the same type of creature reported in Pennsylvania.

Big Foot. *Illustration by Lisa Kulp Good.*

MARYLAND

In Maryland, reports of Bigfoot date back to the early 1900s. Witnesses to a recent sighting near Annapolis included a police officer. All witnesses described the creature as a large, hairy biped that stared at them before walking away. Extremely large footprints were found at the site and were examined to determine if they could have come from a black bear, even though the behavior of the creature is not typical of black bears.

DELAWARE

Although some sources claim that Bigfoot has not been sighted in Delaware, there are others who list confirmed sightings in 2003 and 2004. The 2003 sighting was near Route 1 in Lewes and the 2003 sighting was on Arvey Road in Georgetown.

VIRGINIA

Virginia has a long history of Bigfoot sightings, dating back to the 1880s. The Virginia Bigfoot Research Organization was founded to study sightings in Virginia, and their website, www.virginiabigfootresearch. org/, lists sightings from the 1970s up to the present day. Most of the listed encounters describe tall creatures covered with reddish-brown hair; much like those described in the other Mid-Atlantic states.

TRAVELER'S NOTE

The organizations do not seem to desire to prove the existence of Bigfoot; instead they proceed from an acceptance of their existence, and their main purpose is to make contact with these creatures and then help get laws in place to protect their habitats.

Some other websites that describe sightings in the Mid-Atlantic region are: www.bfro.net/, http://sasquatchwatch.weebly.com/, and www.bigfootencounters.com/.

GIANT THUNDERBIRD
PENNSYLVANIA

The Thunderbird is a giant bird from Native American mythology. The Thunderbird is said to shoot lightning from its eyes and create thunder with the flapping of its enormous wings. This creature, or at least something that looks very much like the description of one, has been spotted in Pennsylvania.

The creature is grayish-black, with a body about five feet long and a wingspan of approximately fifteen feet. Witnesses describe their attention being drawn to the sky by a sound of flapping that was like thunder.

In Jerome Clark's book, *Unexplained!*, he lists three incredible sightings in Pennsylvania. The first was in 1940, when Robert Lyman, author of *Forbidden Land*, saw what he was convinced was a Thunderbird sitting on a road near Coudersport, Pennsylvania. As he watched, the giant bird flew away and he observed its wingspan, which he described as at least twenty feet.

The second sighting was in 1969, when the wife of a sheriff in Clinton County, Pennsylvania, saw an enormous bird fly over Little Pine Creek. She swore the wingspan was as wide as the seventy-five-foot-wide creek!

The next year, several people saw a huge, dark-colored bird whose wingspan was similar to that of an airplane.

Sightings continue to be reported up to the present day. The most popular explanations for these sightings are that it is either a species of giant bird that is not known to scientists or it is a known bird whose size is misjudged or exaggerated.

GOATMAN
MARYLAND

Goatman is a half-man, half-goat creature, similar to a satyr, or the Greek God Pan. There have been sightings of him in the area of Upper Marlboro and Forestville, Maryland, around Governor's Bridge Road, Lottsford Road, and Fletchertown Road. There are no reports of attacks on humans by this creature, but there are cases of missing and mutilated pets and animals that have been attributed to him.

One theory of his origin is that he is the result of experiments done by the Agricultural Department in which they were creating hybrid creatures. Other theorists claim he is none other than the Devil himself.

BLACK DOG
DELAWARE AND MARYLAND

This creature is well-known in certain areas of the UK. The Black Dog, or Black Shuck as he is sometimes called, is a huge black dog, often as large as a small cow, with glowing red eyes. He is not the ghost of a dog, but is a creature unto himself. This dog is seen in the Delaware and Maryland regions of the Mid-Atlantic and is described the same way as he is described in sightings from the UK. Traditionally, the first time you see a Black Dog it is good luck. The second time is bad luck, and the third sighting means you are going to die.

In Maryland, on Highway 12 between Frederica and Felton, a huge dog with red eyes has been reported for over 100 years. Some theorize that he appears most often after fatal accidents on the road as a guide to help the accident victims' spirits to the other side.

Black Dogs appear in *thin* places—places where the veil that separates the physical world from the spirit world is at its thinnest. The dogs serve as guards, much like the mythical Cerberus was a guard of the gates of the Underworld in Greek mythology.

TRAVELER'S NOTE

Highway 12
Between Frederica and Felton, Maryland

THE BLUE DOG
MARYLAND

Referred to as the "Blue Dog of Rose Hill," he is said to be the ghost of a dog belonging to a Revolutionary War soldier named Charles Thomas Sims. Sims and his dog were traveling along Port Tobacco Road after a night at the tavern when they were waylaid and murdered by a man named Henry Hanos, who stole his gold as well as the deed to his home.

For some reason, Hanos buried the gold and the deed under a holly tree near a big rock. When he tried to dig it up later, he was chased away by the ghost of the dog.

According to Olivia Floyd, once owner of nearby Rose Hill mansion and a spy for the Confederacy, the ghost of the "Blue Dog"' haunts the spot every February 8, the date of the murder in 1776. She reported seeing the apparition in an 1897 story in the *Port Tobacco Times*.[3]

The stone has been moved from its original spot, but is still on the same property, and local residents swear the blue dog still protects the deed and the gold buried there. No one has ever reported being able to dig it up, so as far as we know, the treasure is still there.

TRAVELER'S NOTE

Port Tobacco Road
Port Tobacco, Maryland 20677

BULLBEGGAR ROAD
VIRGINIA

Bullbeggars are creatures from English folk lore. It is not clear why a road in Virginia is named for this being, as Bullbeggars were nasty little creatures used to scare children and other impressionable people.

Its name is derived from an old Celtic word *bug* for evil spirit or goblin.[4]

TRAVELER'S NOTE

Bullbeggars Road
New Church, Virginia 23415

CHESSIE
CHESAPEAKE BAY

Chessie is the name that was given to the large, serpent-like creature that has been spotted in the Chesapeake Bay. Theories on what Chessie really is range from it being something as benign as a manatee to the more unusual, which hold that Chessie is a leftover prehistoric water creature. Existing photos show that Chessie is most definitely a large and living creature, but are not clear enough to determine exactly what species Chessie could be.

Most if the sightings describe a long, serpentine creature. The reported length varies from twenty-five to forty feet long. It is seen swimming much like a water snake does, moving its body in a curve from side to side. There are isolated sightings here and there, but there was a huge wave of sightings in the late 1970s and the mid 1980s. Despite all of these sightings, and a similar amount of photos and video, there is still no proof of Chessie's existence.

HORNED SKULLS
PENNSYLVANIA

I first came across this story in a book called *Forbidden Land – Strange Events in the Black Forest*. It was an intriguing tale: During the excavation of a Native American burial mound, two skulls were unearthed that were not only at least seven feet tall, but they also had horns sprouting from their heads. The skulls were said to have been sent to the American Investigating Museum, but no one has been able to locate any horned skulls since.

Did they disappear? Did someone walk off with these unusual artifacts? Most likely, this was just a case of mistaken identity. It may have been that horns had been buried with the skulls or it may have been part of a mask that was buried over the face.

TRAVELER'S NOTE

The skulls were supposedly unearthed in Sayre, Pennsylvania.

WITCHES AND WITCHCRAFT

Today witches are seen as peaceful practitioners of a religion called Wicca. They revere nature and abide by the Law of Three, which holds that anything you do comes back to you times three. They strive to always send out positive energy or magic, so that the positive energy returns to them and they are blessed.

Two hundred years ago, witches were viewed very differently than they are now. Witches were supposed to be able to foretell the future, change shape, raise storms, cast spells, and more. They were assisted by an animal familiar, usually a cat, a bird, or a toad. They assembled in large groups at midnight to worship Satan, whom they had sold their soul to in exchange for their magical powers.

HOW TO BECOME A WITCH

It was not enough to just know some spells and folk magic in those times. In order to be a witch, or so our ancestors believed, one had to be fully initiated by a member of the opposite sex. The initiation takes place in a cemetery during the new moon. The witch begins by renouncing the Christian religion and then follows that by giving herself, body and soul, to the Devil. During the initiation, they are joined by various devils and evil spirits as well as two members of the coven. The deal is sealed by a recitation of the Lord's Prayer backwards. This is repeated three nights in a row. After the third night, the witch must serve her master forever.

These initiation descriptions come mainly from confessions offered under torture and threats, and no descriptions of ceremonies were written by witches themselves. These were recorded by the witchfinders and the Christian Church.

HOW TO FIND A WITCH

The two most common ways back then for finding out whether someone was a witch were by looking for an unusual mark on the suspected witch's body and by ducking. The mark could be anything from a mole to a scar, and even a slight discoloration of the skin could be a witch's mark. Often the mark was tested by inserting a long pin into the mark to see if it would bleed. If it bled, then it was not a witch's mark.

Ducking involved tying the suspected witch's right thumb to her left toe and her left thumb to her right toe. If the suspect sank and drowned, she was innocent. If she floated or swam, she was guilty. This was because water was believed to be so pure it would not accept a witch. Of course, if the water did accept a suspect, she was found to be innocent of the charges. She would be dead, but her soul would be in heaven.

A CAPITAL CRIME

Witchcraft was a crime punishable by death, and was deplored by both Catholics and Protestants. The Mid-Atlantic region was not immune from these unenlightened views, and there were witch trials and executions here, just as there were in Salem, Massachusetts. Areas that were associated with witches have retained some of that unusual and spirited energy. Some of the victims of witch trials and persecutions have been unable to rest. Perhaps they stay in the dark and wild places that are still avoided, in order to clear their names. It may be that they remain for a darker reason. Maybe they remain to avenge the injustices that were done to them in life.

THE WITCHES' TREE
DELAWARE

A gnarled old tree with missing limbs stands alone by a dirt road in Gumboro, Delaware. Local thrill seekers have defaced and hung things from this Witches' Tree, as it is known. It is said that suspected witches were hanged from this tree, which has a definite energy about it.

It is likely that this energy is due to the presence of a dryad, which is a nature spirit that inhabits a tree. When the tree becomes sick or damaged, it hurts the spirit as well. If the tree dies, the dryad dies with it. The dryad of this poor lonely tree must be very forlorn. Instead of spray paint and trash, someone should leave an offering of water.

TRAVELER'S NOTE

Swamp Road
Gumboro, Delaware 19973

WITCHES' HILL
PENNSYLVANIA

This mountain in Berks County, Pennsylvania, was believed to be a place where witches gathered on April 30th to celebrate Walpurgia. Their shadowy forms and strange, unexplained balls of light are still seen there today.

Walpurgia is an event held to celebrate the start of spring. Large bonfires are lit and there is dancing and merriment. These types of celebrations were seen as pagan and evil by the conservative Quakers, Amish, and Mennonite settlers here, so the areas where these rites took place were avoided and given names like "Hexenkopf" (Witch's Head) or Hexendanz (Witch's Dance).

TRAVELER'S NOTE

Hexenkopf Road
west of Allentown in Berks County, Pennsylvania 19529

THE FIRST WITCH TRIAL
VIRGINIA

The first witch trial, well, arraignment, in the colonies occurred not in Salem, but in Virginia in September of 1626. The name of this unfortunate woman was Joan Wright. She was a midwife and knew many folk remedies. Joan was also left-handed, which caused people to distrust her. On three separate occasions, Joan foretold the death of people. This may have been because of her knowledge of folk medicine, or it may have been precognition, or the ability to foresee the future.

29

Suspicion of Joan grew to accusation when a woman who she had helped deliver a healthy baby developed a breast infection and then her husband and baby fell ill as well. She was fined 100 pounds of tobacco and it is not known what happened to her after that. Hopefully, she moved to somewhere her talents would be better appreciated.

KATHERINE GRADY
VIRGINIA

Crossing the Atlantic Ocean in the 1600s was a tricky business. It took at least six weeks on a small, wooden ship. For example, the *Mayflower*, which was an average ship for the time, was 90 feet long and 20 feet wide. This ship carried 102 passengers and 47 crew members.

Living conditions were far from comfortable, even for the seventeenth century. Ships tended to be overcrowded and had no private cabins, no bathrooms, and no water to wash with, unless you wanted to use sea water. Everyone slept below deck, where there was hardly any light or fresh air. Chances are, by the time the voyage was nearing its end, patience was thin and tempers flared.

In 1654, Katherine Grady was traveling on a ship from England to Virginia when a violent storm blew up. Immediately, the superstitious sailors blamed witchcraft. Katherine was an elderly woman who either most resembled a witch or was least likely to put up much of a fight. The captain hanged her during the storm in an effort to stop it. It is unknown whether this ended the storm, but the hanging was reported to authorities when they landed in Jamestown.

MARY DERRY
PENNSYLVANIA

High up on a hill above Uniontown in Fayette County, Pennsylvania, lived an old woman. She was the one that locals sought when they needed a cure or a hex. She could tell the future with her "erdspiegel" or witch's looking glass. Existing descriptions of her vary widely, from a very small woman to a very large woman with protruding teeth and a hairy mole on her face. She is also known as Moll Derry, Mary Dell, Moll Wampler, and the Fortune Teller of the American Revolution. She was born about 1765, and lived to the ripe old age of 78. She was feared and respected for her abilities, but it is hard to believe she was such a prodigy that she achieved fame for being the Fortune Teller of the American Revolution. When the revolution started, she was only 10 years old and she was 16 when it ended, but this is the way folklore goes.

POOR POLLY

Mary Derry or Moll Derry is mentioned in conjunction with a local tragedy; the death of Polly Williams. Mary is said to have warned her of her fate at the hands of her lover. Polly was born in 1792 to a poor family in western Pennsylvania. She is described as being fair-haired and beautiful. As a young teenager, she got a job working as a servant for the well-to-do Jacob Moss family. She had such a good nature that she was treated very well by the family and when her own family decided to seek their fortunes farther west, Polly elected to stay with the Mosses.

Part of the reason Polly wanted to stay was that she was in love with the son of the Moss' neighbors, Philip Rogers. Philip led her on for two years, promising to marry her, but continually postponing the date. His family was against such a match, of course.

In 1810, Mrs. Moss noticed that Polly had become withdrawn and sad. What did Polly confide to Mrs. Moss? It is unclear exactly what was said, but after the whole tragedy played out, Mrs. Moss said that Polly told her that Philip was going to kill her. Mrs. Moss, of course, begged her to break off with Philip, but Polly said she couldn't. This is where things get a little murky...

In some versions of the story, Philip had told Polly they were finally really going to be married and so she went off with him. In other versions, they met at their usual meeting place at White Rocks and she told him that she was now pregnant and he had to marry her.

All versions end with Polly dead, in a crumpled heap at the bottom of a sixty-foot cliff. In some versions, she jumped, but in most versions she was pushed. Available records and her tombstone inscription would indicate the latter version. Philip was acquitted of any wrongdoing in her death, but he was convicted in the court of public opinion and had to move away.

Polly was buried in a local cemetery, in the Wilson family plot. She may be buried there, but she doesn't rest. Rock climbers and hikers have reported seeing the ghost of Polly wandering around the cliff.

The ghost of Mary Derry has not been seen, but lives on in local legend and in a poem called "Moll Dell," which one can read in the book *Southwestern Pennsylvania in Song and Story* by Frank Cowan.

He describes the subject of the poem as having inspired such faith in the people of Somerset that "she kept a whole township digging for a gold mine for a lifetime."[5]

Moll Derry was widely known for predicting the future, providing healing remedies and flying through the air on her broomstick. It is likely that she was a practitioner of powwow, a "magico-religious practice whose chief purpose is the healing of physical ailments in humans or animals, although it can also be used to further other ends such as conferring protection from physical or spiritual harm, bring good luck, or revealing hidden information."[6]

MARGARET MATTSON
PENNSYLVANIA

Margaret Mattson went down in history as the accused in the only witch trial in Pennsylvania. She and her husband, Neil, were from Sweden and had settled on a land grant in Eddystone in 1670. The area where they lived is where the Baldwin Building is now. The end of the Mattson property was Simpson Street.

About a decade later, English settlers began arriving in the area and that's when the trouble started. On February 27, 1683, Margaret was put on trial for witchcraft in Philadelphia. She pled not guilty and denied all the charges, which included bewitching cows so they did not give milk. William Penn heard the case and in the end found her guilty of having the common fame of being a witch. Her husband and son posted fifty pounds each to guarantee her good behavior.

Until a short time ago, it was generally accepted that Margaret was an innocent victim of superstition. Then I received correspondence from a man who was descended from Margaret who informed me that Margaret really was a witch, proud of it, and she was not a good witch. It was suggested that she had been compelled to relocate to the colonies in order to escape persecution for her practices.

A BLACK WITCH

Margaret was a practitioner of a Scandinavian tradition called Blakula. According to the *Encyclopaedia of Occultism*, there was an outbreak of action against Blakula practioners in 1669 and 1670 in Sweden, which neatly coincides with the Mattsons' emigration. The accusations against the women were made by children, who said they were carried away nightly to be received by Satan himself. The inquiry resulted in the execution of over twenty women who confessed to doing this. A larger number were subjected to various forms of torture. It is not impossible to think that some of these people may have escaped.

In her new home, Margaret was very isolated until the English settlers arrived. They should be grateful that all they suffered were some cows that didn't produce milk and none of their children reported being given over to the devil!

BEWITCHED?

While I was doing research on Margaret, I had several things happen. First, the file about her disappeared from my hard drive. This happened repeatedly, after which I would recreate the file and save it under various names, hoping for the best. Finally, I just named it witch, thinking it would disappear anyway, and that one stuck for some reason. I had some papers about Quakers and witchcraft in the top section of my desk. Without fail, when I came home, just those papers would be strewn all over the desk and the floor. I tried placing other papers on top of them and the same thing happened. The other papers would be in place, but the Quaker ones would be all over. Finally, as I was working on this section, my Tarot cards fell off the shelf and all over the floor. I picked them up and came back to finish, and my astrological chart CD fell off the shelf. Don't be surprised if, while reading this, you notice some odd things occurring.

SETH LEVIS
PENNSYLVANIA

About a hundred years later, not far from where Margaret Mattson lived, was a trio of witches. The Levis family ran a grist mill in what is now Media, Pennsylvania, and their home used to be where the waterworks is now, on Route 1. Three unmarried sisters lived up the hill from the mill. Common belief was that one of the sisters would enter the homes of sleeping residents during the night, and slip a magic bridle over their head, which would transform them into a horse that she would ride until dawn. The unfortunate victim would wake completely exhausted and "hag-ridden" or "haggard."

This continued until the witch chose to enter the home of Seth Levis. He was able to turn the tables on the witch and forced the bridle over her head, turning her into a horse. In the morning, he put shoes on the witch-horse and used her to plow the fields. When he was finished, he released her and she ran home. The doctor was called to the home of the sisters to treat one of them for strange wounds on her hands and feet, which Seth swore were left from the horseshoes!

MOLL DEGROW
NEW JERSEY

Moll Degrow was the Witch of Gully Road in Woodside, New Jersey. Accused of souring milk of local cows and blamed for a number of unexplained infant deaths, she and the area she lived in were avoided by locals, terrified of her casting her next curse on them. The locals eventually got fed up and decided to rid themselves of her, but she saved them the trouble and died before they could burn her out. She is said to be one of the first people buried in Mount Pleasant cemetery, but there is no record of her grave there. Perhaps it does not matter, since she does not rest. Her spirit is said to wander along Gully Road, searching for her next victim.

MOLL DYER
MARYLAND

Moll Dyer is said to have lived in the area of Leonardtown, Maryland, in the late 1600s. She was believed to be a witch and was chased from her home on a frigid winter night. She is said to have frozen to death on a rock where she stopped to rest. The *Washington Times* has called her "perhaps Maryland's best-known bit of witch lore."[7]

There is a road named Molly Dyer Road, but which came first, the legend or the name? There is no record of a Molly Dyer living in the area. The road name and local legend were the only clues we have to her existence. Moll Dyer's Run was named in a deed from 1857. There were five houses around the run, according to a May 1854 survey of the area, on the east side of Clay Hill Road, which is now Route 5. The road that later became Moll Dyer Road was already there. In 1895, sixty acres of land near Clay Hill Road was called Moll Dyer's Hill, just north of Redgate.

In 1911, a huge boulder was found near Moll Dyer Road which had marks on it. This was believed to be the rock that Moll had rested on during her escape. The rock was placed in front of the old jailhouse, which houses the St. Mary's County Historical Society building.

Moll was not the only witch in Maryland, in 1654; the crew of the ship *Charity* on route to Maryland from England testified about the hanging of passenger Mary Lee for suspicion of practicing witchcraft, according to the Proceedings of the Council of Maryland.

JOHN COWMAN
MARYLAND

In 1674, John Cowman of St. Mary's County was arraigned, convicted, and condemned for witchcraft, conjuration, or enchantment upon the body of Eliza Goodall, according to an 1885 edition of the *Baltimore Times*.

REBECCA FOWLER
MARYLAND

On October 9, 1685, Rebecca Fowler was accused of "being led by the instigation of the Divell [to practice] certaine evil and diabolicall artes called witchcrafts, inchantments, charmes, and sorceryes"[8] against a laborer named Francis Sandsbury and others whose "bodyes were very much the worse, consumed, pined, and lamed."[9] She was found guilty of "certain evil and diabolical arts called witchcrafts, enchantments, charms [and] sorceries."[10] (Rebecca was the only person ever executed in Maryland for witchcraft.)

DELAWARE WITCHES

KAREN SVENSSON

Delaware was home to three witch trials, two under Governor Printz, and one under Willliam Penn. In 1652, governor of what was then the New Sweden colony, Governor Printz seized the plantation of Lars or Lasse C because he found Lars and his wife, Karen, guilty of witchcraft. (It is more likely that the governor just wanted their plantation, otherwise why would he have allowed them to live?) Surely, if they were witches, they would have been able to exact some revenge on him for taking their property.

Under English rule, a woman was "taken to court on charges of bewitching her neighbor's livestock."[11] Bewitched livestock behaved strangely: Cows stopped giving milk, refused to eat, or leapt into the air as they died. Bewitched horses became ill, foamed at the mouth, stopped eating, or ran around as if they were insane. It is not known what became of Karen.

GRACE SHERWOOD

Grace Sherwood was attractive, knowledgeable about herbs, and wasn't afraid to stand up for herself. So when hogs and cattle fell sick, crops were blighted, and the populace was plagued by a series of bad storms, they blamed Grace Sherwood. She was questioned and examined. Two witch marks were found on her body but she defended herself and demanded a fair trial. She agreed to be ducked in the Lynnhaven River, near what is now known as Witchduck Point.

On the appointed day, they tied her thumbs to her toes and threw her in the river. Somehow she was able to free herself and swim to the surface. Of course, this just proved she was in league with the devil, so she spent several years in prison.

It was thought that the evidence against her was vague, and had been started by a couple that she had successfully brought a charge of assault against, so when she was released, the governor helped her regain her property. In 2006, the governor officially pardoned her.

Grace Sherwood, or the Witch of Pungo, as she is sometimes called, returns in spirit form every July to visit the place where she was ducked. Her soul is seen as a bright white light that floats across Witch Duck Bay.

WITCHES TODAY

There are many witches and covens throughout the Mid-Atlantic region today. Some are solitary practitioners and others belong to groups. Most of the people who follow the "Old Religion" are members of mainstream society. Wicca and other Neopagan groups have been recognized by governments in the U.S. and Canada and given tax exempt status. Wiccan priests and priestesses have been given access to penitentiaries in both countries, and the privilege of performing handfastings/marriages. On March 15, 2001, the list of religious preferences in the U.S. Air Force Personnel Data System was expanded to include Dianic Wicca, Druidism, Gardnerian Wicca, Pagan, Seax Wicca, Shamanism, and Wicca.

HEXES, JINXES, AND CURSES

A hex is a spell and can be positive or negative. The word comes from the German word for witch, "hexe." The word hex is commonly used in Pennsylvania in the phrase "hex sign." These are symbolic signs placed on or in homes and buildings and are believed to help with luck, health, or even protection from lightning.

A jinx is a run of very bad luck that is caused by a curse or by making overly confident statements about a future event or calling attention to a run of good luck. For example, a person may say something like, "We are winning the game!" When this statement is followed by a loss, it is said that the statement put a "jinx" on the game. Knocking or touching wood after uttering one of these statements is believed to keep the jinx away.

A Traditional Hex sign by Zook.

A curse is an evil spell cast on a person, place, or object and is meant to cause harm or even death to whomever encounters it. A famous example is the Curse of the Pharaohs, which was placed by the Egyptian priests to cause harm and misfortune to anyone who disturbed the rest of any of the Pharaohs.

CAPE HENLOPEN'S CORPSE LIGHT
DELAWARE

Cape Henlopen is host to what some locals call the "Corpse Light." It is a phantom light that ships easily mistake for a lighthouse. The first tragedy happened in 1655 when the captain of the *Devonshireman* steered the ship towards the light and crashed into the rocks, resulting in the loss of nearly 200 lives.

The Corpse Light is said to be a Native American curse of death to white men, placed when British soldiers murdered a group of Natives at a wedding. In support of this story, in 1800, a lone brave was seen standing on a rock, staring out to sea right before an excursion barge wrecked on the rocks, killing many of those aboard. In 1980, the U.S.S. *Poet*, a 12,000-ton grain carrier, vanished without a trace near the coast here.

TRAVELER'S NOTE

Lewes, Delaware
www.destateparks.com/park/cape-henlopen/index.asp

CURSED WAND
NEW JERSEY AND DELAWARE

Stephanie collects witches and anything related to them. This is what led her to purchase a witch's wand from E-Bay. The seller claimed the wand was fashioned from a branch of the most haunted tree in New Jersey, which grew in an equally haunted cemetery. It was eighteen inches long, topped with a skull wearing a witch's hat.

The wand arrived and she added it to her collection. She put it in her room and she felt it "just stared at her." Two weeks later, her favorite cat died. Three weeks later, another of her cats died. A third cat became so sick she almost died.

Then her favorite Christmas ornament, which she had anchored to the tree, was found smashed on the floor and she found her grandmother's precious diamond ring inside the trash can. Following this incredible run of very bad "luck," her dog had a stroke and then she herself injured her back so badly that she was out of work for nine weeks.

Her mother then said, "Get rid of that wand!" So, she threw it out in the trash.

The bad luck, however, continued and spirit activity started in her house. She heard disembodied voices at all hours, smelled cigar smoke, and never really felt like she was alone in her home. Desperate, she visited a witch shop in Dover, Delaware, and was given direction on a house

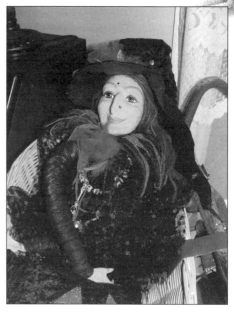

One of the Witches in Stephanie's collection.

cleansing she could do to get rid of what she believed was a curse. She followed the directions and things lessened, but there was still spirit activity in her home. Fortunately, the curse part of whatever had been going on seemed to have run its course.

We feel that the spirits that stay there now are of a benevolent and protective nature, perhaps guarding against any negative energy coming into the house.

THE JINX HOUSE
PENNSYLVANIA

The house in Pomeroy seemed like a dream come true for Tracey and her family. The four-story Victorian home was beautiful and spacious enough for her children to each have their own room. In addition, there was a formal living room, fireplaces, built-in shelves and cabinets, and even a big room they could turn into a playroom! The best thing was the rental price, which was less than she was thinking she would have to spend for a house – especially one of that size. They couldn't wait to move in.

Shortly after they got settled, they underwent personality changes. Both Tracey and her husband became short-tempered and confrontational towards each other. The children refused to stay in the playroom. No matter what she did to brighten it up, the house always seemed dark. Things got worse.

One night, she and her husband were awakened because their bedroom had become unnaturally cold. They could actually see their breath! To their horror, they then heard slow and steady footsteps walk up the hallway and into their bedroom. It was clear there was no living human making those sounds. Then her husband lost his job and their finances went downhill. It wasn't until something pushed her on the attic stairs, causing her to lose her balance, fall, and break her foot that she really began to think there was some kind of jinx on the house.

She called a friend of hers who called me and asked me to come and see if I could give them some insight into what was going on in their house. When I arrived at the house with two other women, another psychic and an investigator, they were all standing outside, reluctant to be in the house. Tracey told me that they were moving because they couldn't take anymore.

We were only in the house a short time when the other psychic began to be affected by the atmosphere and turned on us, saying she didn't want to be around us anymore. She left the house followed by the investigator, who returned to me a short time later, reduced to tears by whatever the psychic had said to her. This was so out of character for this psychic I was beginning to get worried about which of us might be affected next.

I walked up to check the attic and suddenly something pulled my ankles out from under me. I fell heavily on the stairs and only avoided falling down the whole flight by throwing my arm out to grab the banister. That was enough for me. Whoever was in there clearly wanted to be left alone. Tracey later told me that those were the same steps she had been pushed down. I did a walkthrough of the rest of the house and we held a communication session which confirmed my feeling that the spirits there wanted us to leave them alone.

Doorway to the attic...
and the haunted stairs.

I kept in touch with Tracey and she said that when they moved away the change was like night and day. Their bad luck disappeared and their financial problems cleared up. She still lives in the area and drives by the house occasionally. New people live there now, but the "for rent" sign is frequently seen in the front window. She swore the last time she drove by she felt like something in the house knew she was there and watched her drive by.

TRAVELER'S NOTE

So, if you are looking for a house to rent in Pomeroy, Pennsylvania and you find a gorgeous Victorian home offered for an extremely low price, be careful. You might be looking at the Jinx House.

CURSED MINE
MARYLAND

The mine was opened in 1865 after a Union soldier camped near Great Falls saw some gold in a stream. Everything went well for over forty years until a run of bad luck led to the mine being closed. First, there was an explosion when a miner set his helmet with a candle lamp down next to a box of dynamite. One miner was killed. After that, things got worse.

A horse refused to enter the mine. When it was brought to the gate it would rear and paw at the air. The miners began to hear unexplained footsteps and knocking and hammering sounds behind them. Stories spread of "Tommy Knockers" in the mine. Tommy Knockers are the ghosts of dead miners that return either to warn of impending danger or foretell the death of whoever hears them. The last straw was when a night watchman claimed to see what he described as a demon enter the mine. He promptly quit. Men began refusing to work in the mine as word of the curse spread and it was closed for good in 1908.

CATAWBA
NEW JERSEY

South Jersey is full of little ghost towns that sprung up around the iron-making, shipbuilding, and brick-making industries. Some of these endeavors failed shortly after they were formed and now it is not unusual to find abandoned mill walls and foundations of long-forgotten homes in the Pine Barrens. Most of these places are just interesting memorials to long dead hopes and dreams, but one of these places is said to be jinxed.

That place is Catawba, New Jersey, about three miles south of Mays Landing. George West was a Methodist minister, and he and his wife came to southern New Jersey to build a church and begin a settlement around it. They started building a huge mansion in 1813, and donated an acre of ground for the building of a church and burial ground. In less than fifteen years, George, his wife, and three of their four sons, would be dead and buried.

No one is sure what killed the family. It started on May 14, 1826, when their 14-year-old son, Thomas Biddle West, fell ill and died in a little over two days. Not much was thought of this, other than the seemingly healthy boy had been struck down suddenly, and the family went about their business and the little town of Catawba continued to work at the shipbuilding business that provided its livelihood.

Three years later, their 19-year-old son, James, passed away suddenly from some kind of illness. Again, no one thought much of it except to think that perhaps the West family was having a run of bad luck, or a jinx. Nine days later, George West Junior, age 23, was dead, followed a week later by his father.

Now rumors were probably flying about some kind of curse on the family, as there are no records or rumors of other families being similarly affected. People began to move away when Amy West, the mother, died five days after her husband. One son survived and was then suspected of poisoning his whole family. He apparently packed up under a cloud of suspicion and took off for greener pastures, never to be heard from again. Many of the local residents had worked for the West family, so they too were forced to move and seek employment elsewhere.

The town became abandoned and was avoided by locals, who spoke of a curse or a jinx on the West family. How tragic that they moved there to found Catawba as a fresh start and ended up dead under mysterious circumstances.

INDIAN CURSE ROAD
NEW JERSEY

What started out as a highway designed to save time and cut down on traffic in South Jersey would end up in the middle of a controversy – and a curse! As they were digging to build Highway 55, the workers unearthed evidence of a Native American settlement. Local tribes people and historians called for the work to be halted and it was briefly suspended, but when no evidence of burials was found, they decided to proceed with the construction.

Cursed Highway.

Chief Wayandaga of the Delaware Tribe, spiritual leader of the tribe, and a direct descendant of those people who lived at this site, said that he prayed to the Great Spirit and his ancestors for the site to be protected. He insisted that a burial site would be within a short distance of the village and the ground was sacred. Anyone who disturbed it would be cursed. The chief said he warned the workers about what might happen, but they didn't believe him.

Then the accidents began. One of the workers was run over by an asphalt roller. Another was blown off a bridge overpass and fell to his death. Then an inspector dropped dead from an aneurysm at the site. Finally, a vehicle carrying some Department of Transportation workers, caught fire and exploded. The curse even seemed to extend to the families of the workers, who began to experience sudden and unexplained deaths and cancers.

Today, the road is a busy highway near Deptford, New Jersey. Chief Wayandaga claims that until the road is relocated, there will continue to be deaths associated with it. I have not read any accounts of unusually high numbers of accidents there, so maybe the curse has worn itself out or perhaps it is just waiting for an opportune time to strike again.

THE CURSED TOMBSTONE
PENNSYLVANIA

On a quiet country road lies a lonely Quaker cemetery and a long-abandoned meeting house. The setting is beautiful and relaxing. One would never think this tranquil plot, used by peaceful Quakers, would harbor a curse. But it does. The tombstone in question belongs to Ella Mae Lynch and William J. Lynch. The inscription on their stone reads,

> Remember youth as you go by, as you are now, so once was I, as I am now so you shall be, prepare for death and follow me.

It's said that if you read the inscription you will be cursed with bad luck, death, and any manner of things in between.

The Cursed Tombstone.

Various reports of ghostly activity are associated with the entire cemetery; there are a number of anomalous photos and EVPs that have been captured here. Some visitors have been touched by frigid, unseen hands and others have had trouble breathing there. I could find no reports of anyone being felled or otherwise affected by the curse, but still, when I went to visit the cemetery I hesitated to speak the inscription aloud – well, for about a second. I then read it aloud, touched the tombstone and even walked around the grave.

Despite having done all of the things involved to activate the curse, I cannot think of one thing that happened to me that I would associate with being cursed. Either my guides are doing a great job of protecting me or the combination of things I did worked together to keep me from getting cursed. Perhaps that was the mistake others made in only doing one of the three things said to invoke the curse.

SPIRITUALISM
NEW YORK

Spiritualism is a belief system that centered around communication with spirits of the dead. It first came to popularity in the 1850s when Margaret and Katie Fox claimed to have communicated with the spirit of a murdered peddler who was said to be buried in the basement of their Hydesville, New York home. Margaret and Katie were the first modern mediums; people who spiritualists believe have the ability to communicate with spirits of the departed.

The spirit of the peddler first communicated with them through knocking or rapping noises that emanated from the floors and walls of the rooms in their home. As they rose to popularity many other people also began to claim to have the ability to communicate with spirits and Spiritualism was born.

45

PHILADELPHIA, PENNSYLVANIA

Philadelphia was a center of culture and commerce in nineteenth century America, so it naturally became a center for spiritualism as well. Among the famous spiritualist mediums and photographers was Jay J. Hartman, who was one of the few spirit photographers never found to be committing fraud. His studio was at 831 Vine Street.

THE WHITE DOG CAFE
PENNSYLVANIA

The White Dog Café at 3420 Sansom Street in Philadelphia was once the home of Madame de Blavatsky, founder of the Theosophical Society. Theosophists believe "that we live in a purposeful universe, that human existence has deep meaning, and that we are responsible for our thoughts and actions."[12]

While living on Sansom Street, Madame Blavatsky contracted a serious infection in her leg. She claimed to have undergone a "transformation" during her illness which inspired her to found the Theosophical Society. In a letter dated June 12, 1875, she described her recovery, explaining that she ignored the doctors and surgeons who recommended amputation. She is quoted as saying "Fancy my leg going to the spirit land before me!" She had a white dog sleep across her leg by night, which is the source of the café's name.

TRAVELER'S NOTE

3240 Sansom Street
Philadelphia, Pennsylvania 19104
http://whitedog.com/university-city.html

Theosophist Lodges

There is a Theosophist Lodge in Philadelphia and another in Bethesda, Maryland.

United Lodge of Theosophists
1917 Walnut Street
Philadelphia, Pennsylvania 19103
215-563-4692
www.ultphiladelphia.org

United Lodge of Theosophists
4865a Cordell Avenue
Bethesda, Maryland 20814
301-656-3566
www.ultdc.org

MUSEUM OF THE MACABRE
PENNSYLVANIA

This Museum is based in Philadelphia and has a traveling exhibit called "An Evening with the Spirits" that can be booked through their website, www.museumofthemacabre.com. Representatives from the museum will bring artifacts from their exhibits, including talking boards, spirit photographs, and more, which can be examined by attendees. The staff shares their knowledge of ghosts, séances, and spiritualism during the presentation.

TRAVELER'S NOTE

The museum exists right now as an online location, but will be opening soon at a location in Philadelphia.

THE OUIJA BOARD
MARYLAND

Although some claim that its origins lie in ancient civilizations, the Ouija Board, as we know it, was a truly American invention, manufactured in our own Mid-Atlantic region.

Using a Ouija Board in a traditional seance room.

The first patent, filed on May 28, 1890 and granted on February 10, 1891, lists Elijah J. Bond as the inventor and the assignees as Charles W. Kennard and William H. A. Maupin, all from Baltimore, Maryland. Kennard's partners pulled out of the business in a little over a year, but the company went on until 1898 when William Fuld and his brother, Isaac, who had been employees of the company, became the manufacturers. It started out as a toy meant to be used by children, but was quickly adopted by Spiritualist circles as an easy method for contacting the other side. The best thing about the board was that anyone could do it; you didn't need a medium or any kind of fancy equipment. Since most people now attended at least elementary school in public or private settings, they could read the simple messages that the board spelled out.

William Fuld died in a freak accident at the factory, giving rise to rumors that production of the boards carried a curse of some kind. His children took over manufacturing of the boards until 1966, when the rights were sold to Parker Brothers.

Today many still use Ouija Boards, or a variation of one, in attempts to contact the dead. It is still marketed as a game, and to our knowledge there has never been any conclusive proof of contact with the dead through one of these boards or any other method for that matter.

TRAVELER'S NOTE

For comprehensive history of the Ouija Board, please visit The Museum of Talking Boards at: www.museumoftalkingboards. com/.

THE SPIRITUALIST CHURCH TODAY

The Spiritualist church is still in existence today, and there are numerous churches throughout the Mid-Atlantic region. They hold regular services, which include an opening prayer, hymns, an address, and demonstration of mediumship.

Spiritualists believe that when we physically die, some part of our essence or personality survives and continues to exist and desire interaction with the physical world. They practice mediumship in order to provide a connection between these spirits and their living loved ones. There are spiritual mediums and physical mediums. Spiritual mediums communicate with spirits by forming a connection from their mind to the spirit. They are then able to pass on messages from the spirits to those in attendance.

Physical mediums produce physical effects, such as rapping, knocking, smells, ectoplasm, and apports among other things. Ectoplasm is a substance that emerges from the body of the medium during a trance. It is taken as physical proof of a spirit presence. Apports are actual items that appear during the trance. These apports can be anything from a small flower to a large stone.

TRAVELER'S NOTE

A Few Spiritualist Churches:

Church of Eternal Life, NSAC
243 West Olive Street
Westville, New Jersey 08093
www.njcoel.org/

First Spiritualist Church of McKeesport
809 Locust Street
McKeesport, Pennsylvania 15132
www.firstspiritualist.org/

Getter Memorial Church, NSAC
1123 Oak Street
Allentown, Pennsylvania 18102
getter@entermail.net

Second Spiritualist Association
423 South Broad Street
Philadelphia, Pennsylvania 19147

DEVILISH DESTINATIONS

Does the devil himself walk the Mid-Atlantic region? There are enough places named after the devil that it would seem that he did at one time. These areas all contain an unusual and disconcerting energy.

DEVIL'S HALF ACRE
PENNSYLVANIA

This area and the old tavern there have been completely restored and are now quite beautiful; the name is the only clue to the land's unseemly past.

This patch of land is located in Solebury Township, on River Road. It got this creepy name during the building of the Pennsylvania Canal. The canal construction was begun in 1829 and was built, without machinery, mostly by Irish immigrants. Digging and building the canal was hard and the workers looked forward to their down time at the local tavern. This popular tavern was what is currently called the Indian Rock Inn.

The spooky legends that surround this now- charming riverside inn are that the ghosts of canal workers killed in brawls are buried on the property and still walk the grounds.

TRAVELER'S NOTE

The Indian Rock Inn
2206 River Road, Pennsylvania Route 32
Upper Black Eddy, Bucks County, Pennsylvania 18972
Phone: 610-982-9600
http://indianrockinn.com/

JERSEY DEVIL
NEW JERSEY

I was sitting around a campfire somewhere in southern New Jersey the first time I heard about the Jersey Devil. I was with my family and we were telling scary stories. Of all the stories told that night, this is the only one that I remember. It terrified and also fascinated me.

A long time ago a woman named Mrs. Leeds had twelve children. When she became pregnant with her thirteenth child, she cursed it, saying, "Let the devil take it." When the baby was born, he transformed into a creature ghastly in appearance looking much like the devil. He let out a loud screech towards the midwife. As she watched in horror, two leathery wings began to grow from his back and he flew out the window.

The Jersey Devil. *Illustration by Lisa Kulp Good.*

Since that day, the creature has terrorized the Pine Barrens and surrounding regions. He has the head of a ram, wings of a bat, and the body and hooves of a horse. Sounds like some kind of strange witch's brew ingredients, but this is how the creature was described by those who have seen it. The Jersey Devil has been sighted in the Pine Barrens of Southern New Jersey and all over the surrounding Mid-Atlantic region.

There really was a Leeds family living in Egg Harbor, New Jersey. Daniel Leeds is listed as the head of the household. He married twice, first to Susanna Steelman and then to Rebecca Steelman, who appears to be Susanna's sister. The children born to Susanna were Dorcas, Rachel, and Andrew. His will mentions his wife Rebecca and three daughters, Susanna, Dorcas, and Rachel. There is no way that this adds up to twelve, and definitely not to thirteen children.

According to the website, njdevilhunters.com, the Jersey Devil may be Smith J. Leeds, who is listed as having died within the first two years of life. Is it possible that there were thirteen pregnancies? Infant mortality rates were very high and there may have been stillbirths and miscarriages not recorded in history. A high number of these unfortunate events may have even led the family or the neighbors to believe the Leeds family was cursed. The first sighting of the creature, around the time of yet another stillbirth in the Leeds family, could have provided the connection between the family and the creature, and the legend would have been born.

So is there a Jersey Devil? The sheer number of reported sightings would seem to indicate that there is something out there. Next time you are traveling through the Pine Barrens or sitting around a campfire in South Jersey, keep an eye on the woods around you. You just might see New Jersey's own devil!

TRAVELER'S NOTE

Visit the Pine Barrens in New Jersey.

THE DEVIL'S HOLE
PENNSYLVANIA

This cave is also known as Durham's Cave. The cave, once an important site to the Lenape Indians, was slowly demolished and its limestone burned to make fertilizer and later to feed nearby iron furnaces. What little still remains is located on private land, and is inaccessible to visitors.

Over the years, many unruly children were brought to heel by the threat of being placed in this cave. It was said the devil himself resided there. Local residents also attributed runs of bad luck to the proximity of this cavern. Bad luck could be anything from a husband coming home late and drunk every night to cows giving bad milk.

TRAVELER'S NOTE

Visit Durham Township in Bucks County, Pennsylvania.

THE GATES OF HELL
PENNSYLVANIA

Did you know the Gates of Hell were located in Philadelphia? They are – at the Rodin Museum! This huge sculpture is one of only a few casts of the original work, which is on display at the Musee Rodin in Paris.

The work was inspired by *Dante's Inferno* and contains sculptures of many figures in various states of damnation and torment. The tortured figures seem to reach out for something, perhaps a savior that is not there. Several of the figures featured in this sculpture were later recast as individual works of art by Rodin.

This huge sculpture was Rodin's obsession for the rest of his life and he worked on it for thirty-seven years, until his death in 1917. Some believe he felt this work, which was originally intended to be the doorway for the Decorative Arts Museum in Paris, would define him as an artist.

Why would he choose such a subject for a doorway? Perhaps *Dante's Inferno* spoke to him about his own experience and struggle to complete this project, which was a very important commission for him.

DEVIL'S DEN
PENNSYLVANIA

Devil's Den is the nickname for a terrain feature south of Gettysburg, Pennsylvania, that was the site of fierce fighting at the Battle of Gettysburg during the American Civil War.

Many spirits of soldiers have been seen here in this rugged terrain that was held and fiercely defended by the Confederate troops. Perhaps this is because of the violence that happened here or maybe because Devil's Den hasn't changed much since the Battle of Gettysburg.

During the battle, Confederate sharpshooters holed up in the crevices of Devil's Den and this enabled them to target the Union troops on the other side of the valley on Little Round Top. For weeks after the battle, dead Confederates littered the fields behind Devil's Den. Some of their bodies were

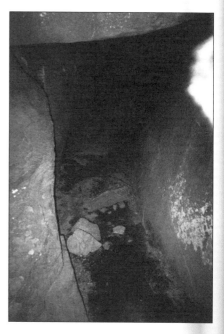

Mist forms in the Devil's Den.

pulled from where they fell and placed in positions where there would have been snipers in order for enterprising photographers to get good shots.

TRAVELER'S NOTE

Visit Gettysburg Battlefield Park, Gettysburg, Pennsylvania.

THE DEVIL'S POOL
PENNSYLVANIA

A secluded, rocky area of the Cresheim Creek, the Devil's Pool is a very deep spot created by a little waterfall. Unfortunately, its seclusion means that it is frequently littered with trash and graffiti from visitors with little respect for nature or others who may want to enjoy a visit to see the location.

The name comes from its unusual depth and perhaps from the quiet presence that seems to occupy it – not so devilish. The presence seems protective, almost nurturing. It is my opinion that the spirit presence is actually a nature water spirit; an undine.

Undines resemble humans in appearance and often inhabit waterfalls and rocky pools like the Devil's Pool. The undines are likely quite dismayed at the state the pool is sometimes left in.

TRAVELER'S NOTE

Located at Cresheim Creek, right before it meets Wissahickon Creek.

THE DEVIL'S TOWER
NEW JERSEY

In the early 1900s, a wealthy man named Manuel Rionda built a beautiful estate, complete with an observation tower, in what is now Alpine, New Jersey. The tall tower afforded a view of the estate with New York City in the distance. Manuel's wife, Harriet, is said to have loved to spend time in the tower, viewing the landscape. Legend has it that one day, while enjoying the vista, she also saw her husband with another woman. She was so distraught she threw herself from the tower.

Now the once-beautiful centerpiece of the landscape is known as the Devil's Tower. Some say that if one walks six times backwards around the tower, the ghost of Harriet will appear. Other versions of the legend claim that instead of Harriet, the devil will appear, hence the name, Devil's Tower.

Unfortunately for the legend lovers, Harriet died of natural causes in 1922, and is buried in Brookside Cemetery in Englewood, New Jersey. Manuel lived for another two decades and is interred next to his wife. How and why the tower became associated with the devil is not known. The only thing that happened in the tower's history is that, after Harriet died, she was buried in a mausoleum next to the tower. She and her sister, who was also buried there, were removed when Manuel died to be reburied with him. It is known that disturbing someone's burial site often releases energy as well, many times resulting in a haunting. Is this the case at the Devil's Tower? There's one way to find out for sure, if you are brave enough to try!

TRAVELER'S NOTE

Rio Vista, Alpine, New Jersey.

HAUNTED PLACES

Some haunts are landmarks, others are historical places or even private homes. What ties them together are their ghostly inhabitants. Many times the reason for the ghostly presence is found in the history of the place, but other times the reason for the haunting is related to an object or a person. The long history of the Mid-Atlantic region provides the background for many haunted places and people.

HAUNTED TOWNS
NEW CASTLE, DELAWARE

"First it was Dutch, then it was Swedish, then it was English" is how our ghost tour guide summarized the early history of New Castle, Delaware. The historic district has old cobblestone streets and many colonial houses that date back to the early 1800s, of which quite a few are haunted.

LESLEY MANOR

Now a private residence, this used to be a bed and breakfast called Fox Lodge. It is a very Gothic-looking Victorian house that was built in 1855 for Dr. Allen Voorhees Lesley. There are rumors that it was a stop on the Underground Railroad, due to the presence of a false floor between the third and fourth floors, leaving enough room between for someone to hide.

It seems that Dr. Lesley never left his beautiful home. A man has been seen on the second floor, sitting in front of the fireplace. Descriptions of him by witnesses sound strikingly similar to what Dr. Lesley looked like.

THE GREEN

The Green behind the courthouse was the site of slave auctions, public floggings, and executions. This was the site of the first and only woman ever strangled and then burned at the stake for a crime in America. It happened in 1731. Her name was Catherine Bevan, and she was accused of murdering her husband with the help of her hired hand, who was her lover. First, they had tried to poison him, and when that failed, her lover beat him while Catherine strangled him with a handkerchief. Unfortunately for her, she was not killed by the rope strangulation, so she was set on fire while still alive and died in terrible agony. On windy nights you may hear the whisper of her voice across the green. She sighs, "I'm innocent."

The Green was the site of a horrific execution.

TRAVELER'S NOTE

New Castle County, Delaware 19720

AMSTEL HOUSE

The Amstel House used to be a private home but is now a museum. It is haunted by a woman in a blue dress who gazes out the second-floor corner window. They are not sure who she is. The history of the house gives four possible women who could be the lady in the blue dress.

The first possibility is Elizabeth Van Neuvenigh Bird Burnham. She was married to a man named John Burnham and they lived in the Amstel House in the 1870s. They had three children; John, Lucy, and Elizabeth. Her daughter, Elizabeth, passed away at the age of 15 from tuberculosis, which ran rampant at that time. Her daughter, Lucy, died at an even younger age of the same disease, and finally her husband also succumbed in 1878. When John died, she was not able to keep the house and sold it. It went through various hands and was many things, from apartments to a barber shop.

The other candidate for the lady in blue is Elizabeth Burnham, who died at 15. Not much is known about her, other than her death, which was undoubtedly traumatic for her parents.

The third candidate is Elizabeth Nixon VanDyke, who died in childbirth bearing her first child, Rachael. She had only been married to her husband, Nicholas, for a year. He moved into the Amstel House after her death, but it is thought that she may have followed him there.

The last candidate is Anna Finney, one of the first residents of Amstel House. Her father was the one who built the house. She was in love with a British soldier who went to fight in the French and Indian War. Sadly, he was killed near Braddock, Pennsylvania, and when Anna heard the news, she shut herself in her room and swore that she would never marry. She did get "married off" to her cousin, Jonathan Finney.

Caretakers, volunteers, and visitors have all reported hearing phantom footsteps and seeing shadows flit by out of the corner of an eye and of course, the "woman in blue" looking out of the second-floor window. One volunteer even heard singing coming from the house early in the morning when no one was there.

When we were in the bedroom where the lady in blue is seen, we felt the presence of a male spirit. Fred, a psychic who had accompanied us on the tour, felt that he had something wrong with his legs, while I saw a man who seemed in the prime of his life. Was this John Burnham or one of the Finneys? From the way the man I saw was dressed, I would say he was one of the Finneys, either John or David, as he was wearing typical eighteenth-century clothing. The man that Fred was picking up on may have been John Burnham, since he became ill and died there, or it even could have been another resident from a later time.

A lady is seen looking from the window of the Amstel House.

TRAVELER'S NOTE

2 East Fourth Street
New Castle, Delaware 19720
302-322-2794
www.newcastlehistory.org/houses/amstel.html

DAVID FINNEY INN

The property at 222 Delaware Avenue in New Castle, Delaware was built by David Finney in the 1600s. That makes it one of the oldest buildings in New Castle. At one point, recently, this building was used as a restaurant called Jack's Bistro. The staff and patrons there heard footsteps coming from the upstairs when there was no one there. The footsteps were hard enough to shake the glasses that hung over the bar.

They have had complaints about windows opening by themselves on the third floor. One night, the innkeeper tried an experiment. He waited for a night when no one was staying there and he shut all the windows tight. The window that had been found open received special attention in the form of a piece of wood wedged against the bottom sash. He then locked the door to the room behind him and slept in the room next door. The next morning, not only was the window open, but the wood piece was laid neatly on the dresser.

The ghost is believed to be one of the Finneys; perhaps even David Finney himself!

The second-floor windows of the David Finney Inn have been known to open mysteriously.

TRAVELER'S NOTE

222 Delaware Street
New Castle, Delaware 19720

Jack's Bistro has moved from this location, and at this writing, the building is empty. (Please respect this private property.)

JESSOP'S TAVERN

Jessop's Tavern & Colonial Restaurant was built in 1674 and named after Abraham Jessop, a cooper (barrel maker) who started his business in 1724. Today, it is a tavern and restaurant with excellent food and the spirit of a woman that tends to hang around by the fireplace. She has been credited with pulling napkins off the laps of patrons as well as cold spots around the fireplace.

When we were there, we were fortunate to get a seat in the "haunted" spot right in front of the fireplace. The other psychic, Fred, and I immediately became aware of the presence of a woman standing between our table and the fireplace. She didn't touch our napkins, but she gave us the impression that she was very unhappy that we were there. She did not want to talk, it seemed like she just wanted us to leave. Perhaps this is the reason for her occasional napkin trick; she is trying to tell diners that their dinner is over and it is time to go!

Fred and I were unable to get a name for this woman, but she seemed to be dressed in colonial clothing. It could be that she resents the constant intrusion of uninvited guests in her home, especially after what would have been business hours when it was a shop.

A very territorial spirit walks in front of this fireplace.

TRAVELER'S NOTE

114 Delaware Street
New Castle, Delaware 19720
302-322-6111
www.jessopstavern.com/

THE ARSENAL

This was the old arsenal and was used as a hospital during the Civil War. At one time it was even a school. Now it is a colonial-themed restaurant and banquet facility. The ladies room is the most haunted part of the building. The taps turn on by themselves and visitors have seen a woman sitting in a chair by the stalls who suddenly disappears. There are also reports of the wait staff setting up a room for a banquet, leaving the room, and then returning to find that the room has been all messed up.

Which period in its history produced the ghost or ghosts is not known. When I visited The Arsenal, I saw a man lingering outside, on the side of the building next to the Green. At first, I thought he was a server, since he was dressed in colonial-type clothing, but as I watched him, two servers exited through the side door and were wearing completely different clothing from the man I had seen. I looked back to where he had been and he was gone.

So if you are headed over to The Arsenal, don't forget to check around the outside of the building as well.

Here, I saw a ghostly man outside the Arsenal.

TRAVELER'S NOTE

30 Market Street
New Castle, Delaware 19720
302-323-1812
www.arsenal1812.com/

PHILADELPHIA, PENNSYLVANIA

Philadelphia is known as the Birthplace of Independence, since it was here that the Declaration of Independence and the U.S. Constitution were signed. Most people are aware of this very historic square mile in our city and select this as their primary destination, as it should be, but when one finishes seeing the Liberty Bell and Independence Hall, they should consider visiting one of the other, lesser-known, but no less haunting, sites in Philadelphia.

BISHOP WHITE HOUSE

Bishop White House has been called the most haunted house on the Philadelphia Ghost Tour and I noticed it given this title in newspaper articles about haunted locations in the city. Naturally, I was intrigued.

The history of the house doesn't seem to hold any especially violent or macabre events. William White became Bishop White when he was made the first consecrated bishop of the Episcopal Church of America during the American Revolution. He then went on to become the Bishop of the Episcopal Church of Pennsylvania and chaplain to the Continental Congress. Accounts of his life report that he was a benevolent and beloved person who did a tremendous amount of charity work. His home on Walnut Street was built in 1787. The location was selected because it was midway between the two churches he served, and he lived there until his death in 1836.

Today, the house is part of Independence Park in Old City. It is rumored that rangers avoid going into the house alone, especially after dark. Rangers, visitors, and passers-by have all reported seeing shadowy shapes in the house.

The Bishop White House where shadowy figures have been seen outside.

63

In addition to the shadowy shapes, more substantial ghosts have been seen. One is a tall, thin man that has been spotted peering from the third-floor window. This window is in the house's library. After Bishop White died, "part of [his] library was given intact to the Divinity School of the Protestant Episcopal Church and when the house was restored, the room was returned to be reinstalled...150 books from his original library are on loan to the Park Service from the Divinity School."[13] Does he stay to watch over the remainder of his library or did the disruption of the library cause his spirit to become restless?

People have also reported seeing a woman in colonial dress through the first-floor windows when the house is closed. Some believe it to be Mrs. Boggs, the White's cook, laundress, and housekeeper. I feel that this is unlikely, as Mrs. Boggs lived on the second floor and would not have spent a great deal of time in the front rooms facing the street. A good candidate for this ghost is either Mrs. Mary Harrison White, the Bishop's wife, who enjoyed entertaining guests in these front rooms and who died in the house in 1797. The woman could also be "Betsy," short for Elizabeth, the daughter of William and Mary, who took over the household duties after her mother died. She was one of the three White children who survived to adulthood. There were others – the exact number varies between two and five – who died in childhood. Although this was not unheard of, it was likely heartbreaking for the Whites, especially the death of William, who was his father's namesake and the one they had hoped would follow in his father's footsteps.

When the Whites relocated to the new house on Walnut Street, William was 3 years old. Contemporary sources said that he was very close to his father. He died on January 22, 1797, when he was 13 years old. Sadly, Bishop White also outlived both of his daughters, Mary and Betsy.

So who are the shadowy figures seen in the Bishop White House? Some theorize that they may be yellow fever victims looking for the Bishop's neighbor, Dr. Benjamin Rush, who was the most famous doctor in the city, even though his preferred method of treatment was bloodletting. It was he who first recognized the start of the yellow fever epidemic in 1793. He and Bishop White both stayed in the city during the epidemic to minister to the sick, even though most of their friends and associates had fled to country homes.

Today, a garden occupies the place where Dr. Rush's home once stood, so perhaps those in search of help approach the Bishop White House, in search of relief from the ravages of their illness.

Apparently, the Bishop White House is not only haunted by human ghosts! Many visitors have encountered a mewing kitten. The kitten looks solid and real, but vanishes when anyone reaches to pet it.

TRAVELER'S NOTE

309 Walnut Street
Philadelphia, Pennsylvania 19106
Open by tour only.

WASHINGTON SQUARE

Washington Square is said to be one of the most haunted places in Philadelphia. It is one of five original park squares that were planned as part of the city when William Penn surveyed the area in 1682. At that time, the square was named Southeast Square, since Quakers did not believe in naming places after people. Although it was intended for us as a pasture and open green area, it wasn't long before it became a potter's field. It served in this capacity for almost 100 years; from 1704 - 1794. In spite of – or maybe because of – the many graves there, the land was leased in 1766 for use as a cow pasture.

The Carpenter family, prominent Philadelphians, had a family plot in the square's center because the suicide of one of them disallowed her from being buried in their church cemetery.

The Revolution was a busy time for the square; beginning in 1776, the fallen soldiers of Washington's Army were buried there.

Pits 20 feet by 30 feet in length were dug along 7th and Walnut Streets which were then filled by coffins piled one atop another until space in the mass grave ran out. Long trenches the width of the Square were hastily dug on the Square's south side.[14]

John Adams described the atmosphere of the square in a letter dated 13 April, 1777:

I have spent an hour this morning in the Congregation of the dead. I took a walk into the "Potter's Field," a burying ground between the new stone prison and the hospital, and I never in my whole life was affected with so much melancholy. The graves of the soldiers, who have been buried, in this ground, from the hospital and bettering-house, during the course of last summer, fall, and winter, dead of

65

the small pox and camp diseases, are enough to make the heart of stone to melt away! The sexton told me that upwards of two thousand soldiers had been buried there, and by the appearance of the grave and trenches, it is most probable to me that he speaks within bounds. To what causes this plague is to be attributed, I don't know – disease had destroyed ten men for us where the sword of the enemy has killed one![15]

The Walnut Street Jail was across the street, where Penn Mutual is now. British and Hessian prisoners were kept there. If they died, they were buried in the square as well. When the British captured the city in 1777, the jail then housed Patriots.

John Watson interviewed a survivor of the Walnut Street Jail when he was doing research for his "Annalls." The man, Jacob Ritter, said that "prisoners were fed nothing for days on end and were regularly targets of beatings by the British guards."[16] The prison was freezing as broken window panes were more common than whole ones. Cells were full of vermin and filth. The desperately starving inmates ate any mice and rats they caught and when they couldn't catch them, they were forced to resort to "grass roots, scraps of leather, and pieces of a rotten pump."[17] Prisoners died daily. They were then buried across the street in unmarked graves.

The Colonials reoccupied Philadelphia in 1778 and became the jailers at Walnut Street again. Now that the tables were turned; it is unlikely that the British and Hessian soldiers fared well at the hands of their former prisoners. The burial trenches began to include the British and Hessians again.

The next influx of mass, anonymous burials began in 1793 when yellow fever ravaged the city and killed thousands of residents. Fear of contagion meant hasty burials, sometimes of those who had just lost consciousness and were not dead.

In 1825, the square was named Washington Square and made into a park to honor our first president. In 1954, it was decided that a memorial should be placed there in memory of the unknown soldiers buried there. To do this, they needed to exhume the body of a soldier. They disturbed quite a few graves before finding a body that could be positively identified as a soldier. They could not tell if he was a British, Hessian, or Patriot, but the memorial reads:

Beneath this stone rests a soldier of Washington's army who died to give you liberty.

With all that history, you would think that the square would be haunted by a soldier or a plague victim. Although they may be there, and have been occasionally reported, the most often encountered ghost in the square is that of a woman in a hooded cloak.

She is believed to be Leah, a Quaker woman who walked the field nightly to keep away grave robbers. She has been encountered by casual passers-by, ghost hunters, and police officers. It is said that the park has such a reputation that it is avoided by the homeless. One thing is for sure, the square is strangely quiet at night.

Tomb of the Unknown Soldier.

TRAVELER'S NOTE

Washington Square
Walnut and 6th Streets
Philadelphia, Pennsylvania 19106

POWEL HOUSE

This gorgeous Georgian mansion on Third Street was once the home of Samuel Powel, the last mayor of Philadelphia under British rule and then the first mayor of independent Philadelphia.

Today, the house is a museum operated by the Philadelphia Society for the Preservation of Landmarks. They are not only proud of their history, but of their ghosts as well. Their brochure mentions the "things that go bump in the night" there.

In 1965, a historian, Edwin Moore, reported seeing General Lafayette and several other ghosts of Continental Army officers ascending the magnificent mahogany staircase. Moore's wife reported seeing the ghost of a young woman in a beige and lavender gown in the drawing room. I have heard that she saw the woman fanning herself and smiling; others have seen this same ghostly lady stamp her foot twice and then disappear.

Although she often speculated, Mrs. Moore was unable to ascertain the identity of the ghost until she was planning an eighteenth-century costume ball.

The Powel House is home to many spirits

Mrs. Moore wanted an authentic costume for the ball. In the course of her search, she came across a woman who had a genuine eighteenth-century gown available for her to wear. The woman told her it must be fate, because the gown she had was an actual gown worn by Peggy Shippen, the wife of traitor Benedict Arnold, at the last party she attended, which had been held at the Powel House!

68

Mrs. Moore was shocked to see the woman lift a beige and lavender gown, identical to the one she had seen on the ghost, from the storage case. So through a twist of fate, the identity of the mystery woman was revealed. The room that the ghost of Peggy Shippen appears in is the room that is located immediately to the left as you walk in the building. She has been sighted in other areas of the house as well, but this is the most likely place to see her.

The Powel House will always hold a dear place to me as it was the location of my wedding reception. We had heard that the ghostly lady of the house tended to be more active during parties and celebrations, so we thought we could keep an eye open for her. Well, we were so caught up in the day's events that any possible ghosts were far from my mind...until I experienced something unexplainable.

The party planner was calling for my husband and I to go back downstairs for the cutting of the cake, so I went over to where my husband was talking with the last two guests in ballroom. As I caught his arm to tell him we all had to go downstairs, I felt a hand on my back, as if someone was trying to get my attention. I turned, thinking it must be my brother-in law trying to get us to go down for the cake, but there was no one behind me. The room was empty except for us.

After the cake cutting, we were told about another incident that was witnessed by several people. The first people to enter the room where the dessert buffet was set up included my friend, Rich. He said that he heard a noise like plates rattling, so he looked around. The other people in the room heard it, too, and it was one of my husband's relatives who found the source of the sound. On one of the piles of plates, the top plate was shaking violently as if someone was pushing on it. None of the other plates were moving. One of the people touched the plate and it stopped. They let go and that was it; the plate was still.

After dessert, Rich asked me to come and look at a portrait upstairs in the ballroom. He said that he felt the woman in this portrait was the ghost of the house. I looked at it and got one of the strongest and clearest impressions I have ever received. There was a woman there, but it was not her in the portrait. The woman in the portrait was related to her and they closely resembled each other; so much so that they were often mistaken for one another. She wanted us to know that, absolutely, the woman in the portrait was not her.

We went to go ask the caretaker, Del, who looked thrilled with my impression. He had long suspected that one of the ghosts in the house was the lady I described; whose cousin was the woman in the portrait. Just as I said, she resembled her cousin so much that they were sometimes mistaken for twin sisters.

TRAVELER'S NOTE

244 South Third Street
Philadelphia, Pennsylvania 19106
215-627-0364
powelhouse@philalandmarks.org

CITY TAVERN

Completed in 1773, the City Tavern played host to many notable events and people who were instrumental in the founding of our nation. It was the unofficial meeting place for the First Continental Congress, and during the latter part of the eighteenth and early part of the nineteenth centuries, it was frequented by George Washington and others who entertained visiting foreign dignitaries there. As the nineteenth century progressed, the City Tavern began to have a great deal more competition. The building was partially destroyed by a fire in 1834.

The fire is the genesis of the most well-known haunting there. The story is that a wedding party was preparing for their nuptials when someone inadvertently knocked over a lamp. One of the drapes caught fire and by the time the blaze came to the attention of those in the room, it was almost out of control. Many members of the bridal party were not able to escape and burned to death, including the unfortunate bride.

The Rebuilt City Tavern – haunted by a burning bride.

Twenty years later, the building was torn down to make space for shops. As the twentieth century neared the halfway mark, interest was renewed in the historic section of Philadelphia when Independence National Park was created. An accurate rebuilding of the City Tavern was completed for the Bicentennial celebration of 1976.

It is not known whether any of the shopkeepers who occupied the space of the original building experienced anything paranormal there. It is known that when the City Tavern reopened for business, it was found to house some residents from the past.

In the corner, where the fatal fire is thought to have started, it is said that candles will not stay lit. One night when we dined there and were shown to our table near that corner, the host who sat us looked a little confused. When we asked him what was wrong, he replied that the candle was missing from our table. A quick look around the room, which was about half full with diners, revealed that every other table had a candle, whether lit or not, on it!

I asked him if that was a common occurrence there, and he said that it was usual to find the candles in that section out after they had been lit, but he had never experienced a candle disappearing before. He did bring a new candle to our table and we had no problems with it.

On another occasion, we stopped outside the tavern to take some photos of the garden area behind it. The story they tell on the Ghost Tour is that some people have reported seeing a ghostly duel take place there. As I held my camera to take a photo, I felt a horrible pain on my hand. It was so bad I actually dropped my camera, which was thankfully attached to the wrist strap that was still around my wrist.

I thought I had been bitten by a large insect. When I looked at my hand there was a circular red mark on it. I told my husband that it felt like someone had put a cigarette out on my hand. Later that night as we were driving home, he said to me, "Isn't that weird that you felt something burn on your hand and the ghost there burned to death?" I had not connected the two things until he said that, but it was an interesting coincidence.

Some claim that the phantom bride has appeared in party photos, but I have never seen one of these photos. Whether the story of the bridal party is true or not, I feel that there is some presence there that is trying to make sure that the rebuilt City Tavern does not suffer the same fate as the original one.

Next time you are in Philadelphia's Independence Park, stop by and visit the City Tavern. Pay close attention to those staff members walking around in period dress. The next one to pass by may be a true link with the past.

The table with the missing candle.

TRAVELER'S NOTE

138 South 2nd Street
Philadelphia, Pennsylvania 19106
215-413-1443
www.citytavern.com

ST. PETER'S CHURCH

Buried here are some of the movers and shakers of colonial Philadelphia, including Stephen Decatur and Benjamin Chew. In addition to these notables, there are many others whose names are not so familiar. Saddest of all is the unmarked plot that holds the remains of seven Native American chiefs who were stricken with and died from smallpox during a visit to Philadelphia in 1793.

Starting in 1834, a shadowy figure was seen walking through the cemetery and through one of the walls. Some witnesses have reported seeing the shadowy figure standing over the unmarked graves of the Chiefs.

Burial place of the Indian Chiefs.

TRAVELER'S NOTE

313 Pine Street
Philadelphia, Pennsylvania 19106

BETSY ROSS HOUSE

Betsy Ross was born in 1752, named Elizabeth, but usually called "Betsy." She was a fourth-generation American; her great grandfather had settled in New Jersey in 1680, one year before William Penn founded Philadelphia. She was the eighth child of seventeen. Her family was Quaker, and when she eloped in 1773 with John Ross, an Episcopalian, it caused a major upset for her family. Quakers did not accept inter-denominational marriages, and the offending parties were subsequently cut off emotionally and financially from their family and the entire Quaker community.

Her marriage was short – John Ross joined the colonial militia in 1776 and was fatally wounded when an ammunition cache he was guarding exploded. Betsy tried in vain to nurse him back to health, but he succumbed to his injuries. In June of that same year, George Washington asked Betsy Ross to sew the first American Flag.

In 1777, Betsy married again, this time to a sea Captain, John Ashbourn. They had two daughters, but one died in infancy. In 1782, her husband was captured by the British while he was attempting to get supplies for the Colonial Army. He was imprisoned in Old Mill Prison in England. Sadly, he died in March 1782, several months after the British surrender at Yorktown, which was the last major battle of the war. Betsy was told of her husband's death by another sailor, John Claypoole, who had also been imprisoned in Old Mill.

The next year, Betsy married John Claypoole and they had five daughters, one of whom died. Betsy retired in 1827 and moved in with one of her daughters in Abington, Pennsylvania. She died in 1836.

Although "Ross" was her surname for a brief period, it is by this name she is always known. Her house is a popular stop for visitors to Philadelphia.

Phantom sobs have been heard in the Betsy Ross House.

Many visitors have reported seeing the ghost of Betsy seated by the foot of the basement bed. She appears to be crying. She experienced so much loss in her life, I am not surprised! One guide also reported that while in the basement kitchen, she heard a female voice say, "Pardon Me."

Another source for a basement haunting could be that a gift shop employee was said to have been murdered there during a robbery years ago.

TRAVELER'S NOTE

239 Arch Street
Philadelphia, Pennsylvania 19106
www.betsyrosshouse.org/

CARPENTER'S HALL

Built in 1773, this was the site of the First Continental Congress. In addition to being full of revolutionary spirit, this building is also home to a heavy-footed spirit that walks down the upstairs hallway and makes banging noises in one of the rooms.

It is thought that this spirit is the ghost of Tom Cunningham, a Carpenter's Guild member who rented out one of the upstairs rooms in the late 1800s. He perished during a yellow fever epidemic in 1879 and has been heard there ever since.

Carpenter's Hall, the site of banging noises and heavy footsteps.

In 1960, the Philadelphia police investigated loud noises in the attic which had been reported by the building's caretakers.[18] The police arrived; they found nothing, but were repelled by a foul smell from one of the rooms. About fifteen years later, the governor of Pennsylvania held a meeting at Carpenter's Hall and reported "loud voices and the smell of tobacco emanating from the attic."[19]

TRAVELER'S NOTE

320 Chestnut Street
Philadelphia, Pennsylvania 19106

CAPE MAY, NEW JERSEY

The first residents of Cape May were the Kechemeche Indians of the Lenape tribe. The area was purchased from the tribe in the 1630s and then prospered as an English fishing and whaling colony. Back then it was called Cape Island.

In 1766, visitors began to travel to the Cape from Philadelphia and helped make it a summer resort destination. Public tenant houses were built, as well as taverns and private homes. As word spread about the beauty of the Cape, society people from as far away as New York, Washington, and Baltimore began to travel there. Larger hotels were built to accommodate more guests and music pavilions and ballrooms began to appear to provide entertainment for the summer visitors.

Cape May has survived two major fires and at least twice as many hurricanes. It remains a popular resort town today, with visitors from all over the world. One of the fires completely decimated thirty-five acres of the Cape in 1878, and it was rebuilt in the Queen Anne and Gothic Revival styles that we find so charming today.

A visit to Cape May is all it takes for one to see why many of its past residents have decided to never leave.

ELAINE'S BED AND BREAKFAST

I was introduced to this bed and breakfast when doing research with Dinah Roseberry for our book, *Cape May Haunts*. That was the beginning of a long relationship with the Inn and the ghosts there. The most active areas are the bar, the second-floor porch and sunroom, and the second-floor hallway; although the paranormal activity is not confined to any one area as the spirits seem free to roam around the place. The spirits we have encountered there include a young girl that the staff calls Emily, a woman in white, a man in the dinner theater, a cat named Streak, and an Irish maid.

The house was bought for Emily Read by her parents. She was very ill and they felt the fresh air of Cape May would help improve her health. She was unable to walk and used a wheelchair, so her father had an elevator installed for her. The elevator has been removed, but the remnants of it can be seen inside a second-floor closet. It started out as a summer home, but the Reads spent more and more time there, as Emily loved it. It is unknown how old Emily was when she died, some say 18, some say 13, some even younger. We ascertained during several EVP and pendulum sessions held at Elaine's that Emily was 16 when she passed away. What was once Emily's room is now Room 4. Her cure room, where she could take the fresh ocean air, is still there and is part of the room.

The cure room, where Emily spent many of her days.

During one visit, I had the pleasure of staying in Room 3. The stay was marked by a few unexplained events that I attribute to the ghost of the girl they call Emily. While sitting in the sunroom I heard a noise like a squeaky wheel turning. My friend and I went to check and saw that the hallway was empty and the hotel was quiet. We couldn't help but think of the ghost of Emily, who was confined to a wheelchair due to her illness. Was it the squeak of wheels as Emily drew closer to listen to our conversation? Or was it the squeak of the old elevator?

The hour grew late and we decided to go to bed. I knew there was one other occupied room near mine and it was straight across. I was surprised to see a bright light, like the TV was on, coming from under the door of Room 4. Thinking that either the maid had left the TV on or maybe guests had come in quietly while we were deep in conversation, I thought nothing of it until the next night.

That night the room was definitely occupied, as I had met the people who were staying there. As I entered my room, I noticed that although I could faintly hear the TV, there was no light coming from under the door. I bent down to check and was shocked to see that not only was there no light, but there was no way light could be seen from under that door. Each door has a brown strip at the bottom of the door that sits flush with the floor, to keep light from being seen. So what was the light that I saw? I think maybe it was Emily's way of letting me know she was there.

After seeing that there was no light under the door of Room 4, I walked into my room and into a wall of strong floral perfume. I did not have any perfume with me, and could find no source for the smell. Just as I walked back to try and find where exactly the perfume fragrance was, it was gone. My friend was with me, and fortunately, she also smelled the perfume, so I knew it wasn't my imagination. As we stood discussing our plans for the evening, we both saw a bottle of hairspray fly across the top of the dresser! It vibrated a little and then was still. We both stared at each other in shock.

My next stay at Elaine's was no less eventful. We had begun offering an hour-long mini-investigation of Elaine's after hours. The first night was marked by numerous cold spots and sudden spikes on EMF meters that were provided to the participants. One man, who was using an extra-sensitive microphone with headphones, even heard a female voice whisper, "We're still here..." When we were in Emily's cure room, I heard a deep intake of breath, followed by a sigh right behind me. This is interesting, since Emily died from consumption and would have had difficulty breathing.

Any doubts about whether Emily was still there were erased the following night as I was preparing for the Saturday night group of investigators. I had just finished doing a bunch of psychic readings back to back and didn't have as much time as I would have liked to change and organize the investigating equipment.

I entered Room 3, changed, sat down on a chair to change my shoes and then went back into the other room to organize the equipment and check batteries. Now, I was in a heightened state of awareness as a result of having done the readings, so maybe that provided just enough energy for Emily to play a joke on me.

I turned around to leave, loaded down with two bags and a large case, and saw that my slippers, which I hadn't worn since that morning, were now flush against the door. There was no way they could have been against the door, since I had just come in the door, but there they were! Again, I felt it was Emily's way of letting me know she was there.

TRAVELER'S NOTE

513 Lafayette Street
Cape May, New Jersey 08204
609-884-4358

EMLEN PHYSICK ESTATE

There are so many stories about this estate being haunted that I made a point of visiting it during one of my weekends there. It is a beautiful house, lovingly maintained and administered by the Mid-Atlantic Center for the Arts (MAC). The money they get from tours and other events help them to keep the place going, so your visit helps a great cause.

I wasn't sure what to expect, except that I had heard vague rumors of the place being haunted by someone called Aunt Emilie. The house was beautifully furnished and very definitely haunted. Our guide did not talk about the ghost, but he didn't have to. She made her presence known shortly after I walked in the door.

There was a strong impression of a lady in dark Victorian-style clothing walking down the stairs as if to greet us. She followed us through the entire tour, pointing out a decorative bowl that the guide did not mention. I asked about the bowl and he said it had belonged to the family and was a housewarming gift. She seemed to be especially proud of this bowl. I thought it was amazing that something that looked so delicate had survived over a century.

I had heard the stories about Emilie, but felt that the woman who was accompanying us on the tour was Dr. Emlen Physick's mother, Frances Ralston. Her bedroom was the last stop on the tour and she seemed a bit put out that we were in her private rooms, but I feel that she understands that in order to keep the estate up, they must do these tours of her home.

As we left the room, she stayed behind, and I sent out a, "Thank you for your hospitality and understanding," to her. When you visit the house, try and remember to do the same thing. She seemed to lighten considerably after I thanked her. She remarked that so few people today remember to do so.

Aunt Emilie still watches over the Emlen Physick Estate.

TRAVELER'S NOTE

1048 Washington Street
Cape May, New Jersey 08204
609-884-5404

CAPE MAY LIGHTHOUSE

I have heard that all lighthouses are haunted. I cannot speak for all of them but can certainly speak for this one. The most haunted area seems to be the third window well up. I felt the strong presence of a sad woman there and was unsure of who she was until I did some asking around about her. A friend of mine, Carol Sollenberger, told me that in 1993, she spent most of her summer in Cape May. She was going to the lighthouse for her morning beachcombing and saw that the park was full of police. She asked someone what happened and learned that a young woman had gone up to the top of the lighthouse and jumped to her death. Her ghost is seen inside the caged tower that was installed after she jumped. She is seen, too, walking around the base of the lighthouse at dusk and also sitting in the third window up.

Built in 1859 from bricks of the previous lighthouse, the current lighthouse is open for tours, and the climb up the 199 steps, if you are up to it, will reward you with a beautiful view of Cape May from one of the oldest continually operating lighthouses in the U.S. You might even see the ghost of that young woman on the way up!

Cape May Lighthouse was the site of a suicide.

TRAVELER'S NOTE

Lighthouse Point
609-884-8656

PETER SHIELDS INN

I had not visited this inn in years when I was contacted by the Travel Channel about it. It is an absolutely stunning and palatial place right across from the beach in Cape May. The show they wanted to film was called *Ghost Stories*, and it was a program about just that – people who had stories to tell about experiences they'd had at haunted places. The Peter Shields Inn had a tragic and checkered past, the perfect setting for a ghost story.

The Inn was once the home of Peter Shields, a real estate tycoon who had a vision of turning Cape May into another Newport, Rhode Island, a resort town that catered to the wealthiest society families in the nineteenth and early twentieth century. Sadly, his dream was never realized and the failure of his grand Cape May Hotel resulted in his own financial ruin. Even more tragic was the death of his 15 year-old-son, Earle, in a hunting accident in 1907.

Earle had been out all day and was attempting to cross from one boat to another with his rifle. As he crossed, the gun went off and shot him in the face. He was carried to the yacht club and then home, where he remained unconscious until he passed away. His body was brought back to the Shields' winter home in Bryn Mawr, Pennsylvania, but his spirit remained at the summer home.

A tragic accident resulted in the haunting of the Peter Shields Inn.

He appeared to me, still injured, and waiting for his father. The injury he displayed was extensive, with a lot of trauma to one side of his face and neck. My neck actually started to hurt as I stood there, trying to communicate with the teenager. Since he was unconscious when his father arrived, it is my opinion that he was not aware of his father's presence and is still waiting for him. His father's spirit also stays at the summer house where they were once so happy, but he stays mainly on the ground floor, still welcoming visitors to his grand home. I tried to determine why he did not go downstairs to his son and what I got from this sad spirit was that he was not ready for what was in the basement. So, father and son remain in the summer home they once loved, the son waiting for the father and the father unable to face the son.

Earle is often seen here, where he passed away.

The most compelling experience I had here involved, ironically, my own son. My husband and son had accompanied me there for the shoot. By the time we were finished, my son, Liam, wanted only me. I had promised to return and say goodbye to Earle, so I brought Liam to the basement with me. As we entered the area, Liam pointed to the spirit and said, "Boo-boo," and then pointed to his own head and neck. The crew members who were with me were speechless. It was obvious my son was seeing exactly what I had described because he pointed to the same areas on his head where I had identified the injuries I saw.

TRAVELER'S NOTE

1301 Beach Drive
Cape May, New Jersey 08204
609-884-9090
www.petershieldsinn.com

HOTEL MACOMBER

One of the few non-Victorian inns in Cape May, the Hotel Macomber, is no less haunted than its flashier, more ornate neighbors. This hotel was built in the early part of the twentieth century.

A great deal of paranormal activity has been reported in Room Ten. Guests have reported the sound of things being moved around, dresser drawers opening and closing by themselves, and lights turning on and off. Clocks mysteriously start and stop and run fast or slow. Many guests have reported the overwhelming feeling of a presence of someone in the room. The presence is so strong that it is uncomfortable. The activity in this room has been linked to a widow who visited the hotel a few times a year after her husband died. Apparently, she was so happy there, she continued to visit even after she died.

On the main floor of the hotel, there is a less happy ghost. It is said to be a former waitress who choked to death. She is called Lily and is believed to be responsible for the unexplained disappearance of kitchen knives. Lily must have quite a temper because in addition to the disappearing cutlery, she is also believed to be the cause of a bunch of heavy iron pots being thrown from their hooks, although no one was hurt by the flying cookware. One time, Lily did shove one of the staff members into the shelves in a walk-in refrigerator.

One night, while I was on the ghost tour here, we stopped at this hotel. As our guide was explaining that electromagnetic energy is believed to have a connection to paranormal activity, we heard a loud pop and sparks flew from the transformer on the wire connected to the hotel. One of my companions whispered to me, "Did you see that?" No one else seemed phased by it – either that or they were too spooked to mention it. Was it the spirit of Room 10 or was it the more fiery-tempered Lily making her presence known? My feeling was it was the latter. Lily is the spirit I would associate with sparks flying.

You may see sparks fly at the Macomber.

TRAVELER'S NOTE

727 Beach Avenue
Cape May, New Jersey 08204
http://hotelmacomber.com/

SOUTHERN MANSION

This estate was built during the Civil War as a summer home for a wealthy Philadelphia business owner named George Allen. The mansion was inherited by George Allen's niece, Esther Mercur, and remained in the family until the mid 1940s when it was purchased by the Crillys, who turned the palatial home into a boarding house. Over the years, it fell into disrepair and was purchased by the current owners in 1996. They lovingly restored the mansion to its former beauty and opened the Bed and Breakfast as the Southern Mansion.

At the time the mansion was built, the Civil War was raging and Cape May was neutral territory. It was often referred to as "down south up north" because although it is in New Jersey, a northern state, it sits well below the Mason-Dixon line. George Allen owned a hat-making business and had the contracts to produce hats for both the Union and Confederate forces.

Spirits stalk the Southern Mansion.

Many of the photos that hang in the mansion today are of Esther's wedding, which was held at the mansion. It was obviously quite an occasion and must have been one of the happiest days of her life. When there is a wedding at the mansion, it brings back fond memories for Esther and she can't help but make her presence known.

Since Esther is known to be active when there are weddings, we were excited to see that they were preparing for a wedding the day we visited. Last minute preparations were in full swing, including the arrangement of some exquisite floral centerpieces containing birds of paradise. A huge sand castle was being sculpted in the courtyard. The feeling of a presence following us around the mansion, and especially as we passed through the area where most of the preparation was taking place, was unmistakable. I felt the presence was Esther, still watching over the social events that take place at her home.

My feeling was validated as we walked onto the second-floor landing and the presence became even stronger and was accompanied by a strong smell of flowers. Before I could remark on the scent, our guide told us that sometimes visitors smell floral perfume when there are no flowers or perfume in the area. They associate this smell with Esther, who was known to favor gardenia perfume.

An unexplained white orb in Aunt Esther's room.

Her bedroom is now Guest Room 9. Knocking and noises are heard from the room when there is no one there. The atmosphere there was so happy and light that I remarked I found it hard to believe people would say the room was haunted since the energy there just felt so good. As I said this, we heard three loud knocks emanate from the corner as if to prove to us that the mansion is really haunted. I began to take photos in the room and one photo stood out from the others. Subsequent photos showed nothing that could have caused a reflection and did not contain the white spot.

There was one other room where I felt a presence; that was George Allen's room. The energy felt very masculine and heavy, almost overwhelming. I felt as if I were intruding in someone's personal space and cannot imagine being comfortable enough to sleep in that room. Our guide said she did not know of any ghostly activity in that bedroom, but she did state that there have been reports in some areas of a Civil War soldier that fades through walls. He is normally seen in the basement ballroom. We could not see the ballroom because of the wedding preparations. It is possible he came upstairs to make his presence known.

TRAVELER'S NOTE

720 Washington Street
Cape May, New Jersey 08204
www.southernmansion.com/

THE SPRING HAVEN INN

This inn was originally a summer cottage for the Harrison family. It was called a cottage because it could be run by only ten servants. One of these servants seems to have stayed behind, still going about the business of cleaning and polishing.

Current management has seen a shadowy figure going in the servants' door to the kitchen.

A shadowy form is seen entering and exiting Spring Haven.

They have also seen a shadowy figure walking back and forth in front of the buffet, as if she is polishing it. This figure has even been seen on the security cameras in the office. They are not bothered by the spirit, whom they have named Sara, but wish they could get her to dust for real!

When we were called by the manager to see if we could pick up on what they had been experiencing, I sensed the presence of a woman immediately. Almost as soon as I rang the bell, it seemed as if there were someone there, coming to see who was there and if we needed anything.

I saw a woman who appeared to be in her twenties, dressed in a long, dark skirt with an apron. As we began to listen to the experiences they had at the inn, I saw her disappear through a door that I later learned led to the kitchen.

I was drawn to the dining room and had the urge to walk past the buffet and into the back, ending up standing near a small closet. I felt that this was where she stayed to watch the guests in the dining room. She enjoyed being of service and was happy that breakfasts, dinners, and teas were served there in a style that she was accustomed to.

Thought to be the ghost of a servant, a woman is seen pacing in front of this buffet.

They wanted us to check out the upper floors as well and we invited Sara to follow us, but she indicated that she would meet us on the landing as she was not to use the front stairs. Those stairs were for guests.

The second floor had a very light and airy feeling, the Country Victorian room in particular seemed to have a happy feeling, as if children had played and laughed there once. Each room was decorated beautifully and invitingly, and we hoped the third floor would hold even more.

We were not disappointed in the least. The rooms on the third floor were just as nicely decorated, each with its own theme. The Harrison Cottage room attracted me the most, as I felt the presence of a male spirit there. I received two names for him, Steven and Jacob, and I was not sure whether one of them was his name or whether he was asking about these two. Both I and the investigator who accompanied me felt a gentle hand touch our hair in this room. We both felt that this was the man's spirit. I felt that he liked the look of women's hair now, as most of them wear it down, rather than up as it was in his time period.

Both of the spirits seemed very happy there and enjoyed the company of the guests who stayed. The Spring Haven Inn is a great haunted base to explore some of the other haunted places in Cape May.

TRAVELER'S NOTE

623 Columbia Avenue
Cape May, New Jersey 08204
609-884-4948

GETTYSBURG, PENNSYLVANIA

THE ORPHANAGE

Currently the Soldier's museum, this building once housed an orphanage for children orphaned by the Civil War. In its beginning years, it was a happy place where motherless and fatherless children could find sanctuary in a loving and caring environment. That all changed when the kind mistress was replaced by a sadistic and hateful woman named Rosa Carmichael. She had no qualms about chaining children in the basement or tying them to fences in freezing cold and blistering heat.

One of her favorite punishments was locking them in the outhouse. This was ultimately her undoing and salvation for the children because she put a young child in the outhouse on Christmas Eve. His cries were heard by passersby and he was released. Rosa was arrested and charged for the second time with child abuse, but back then it was not a serious crime, so she did not go to jail. She was, however, run out of town. It is not known where she went or what happened to her.

It is known, however, that some spirits of children never left the orphanage. On a recent trip to the Orphanage, I discovered the spirits of two children playing in the basement. One was named James and he hung out towards the back of the basement, which is a cramped and dusty place where I can't imagine spending fifteen minutes, let alone days at a time, which is how long the children were kept there under Rosa's care. James was lingering near the hole where children were placed in cramped darkness without food or water. This area today is difficult to enter, but some people have placed toys in there for the spirits of the children. I climbed through the dust and entered the hole, but did not feel any presences in there. I was relieved to see that no children were stuck in there, unable to move on.

I emerged from the hole and saw James again, still lingering at the rear of the basement. He showed me that he had been kept down there for long periods of time due to his inability to keep still and he occupied himself by drawing pictures in the dirt floor with his finger. He liked the toys that were brought there, but he really wanted a ball and a blanket. He indicated that he enjoyed playing with some of the other spirit children that stayed there and he liked it when children, especially young boys, came to visit him.

There was another little spirit running around the basement next to where we were sitting. She appeared as a little girl with dark wavy hair and pink cheeks. Her cheeks were so pink that I wondered if she was ill. She seemed to be running back and forth, but she walked with a slight limp.

Our guide began using dowsing rods to try and talk to the spirits there and I brought out my pendulum. Both instruments indicated that there was a presence that wished to communicate, but they were unable to settle on a spot where the spirit was located. I felt that was because the little girl, who revealed her name as Annie, was running back and forth as fast as she could, enjoying being able to keep the dowsing rods from settling on a location. She said they just like to play games.

The basement is marked by fluctuating temperatures and cold spots. I took a picture towards a cold spot and got the following result:

A mist forms near the doorway in the Gettysburg Orphanage. Is this caused by one of the spirited children running back and forth?

TRAVELER'S NOTE

The Orphanage is one of the most haunted places in Gettysburg and Ghostly Images Ghost Tours run regular nightly tours from March to November, including access to the most haunted areas of the building.

Ghostly Images of Gettysburg
777 Baltimore Street
Gettysburg, Pennsylvania 17325
717-687-6687
www.ghosttour.net/ghostlyimages.html

GHOSTS OF GETTYSBURG HEADQUARTERS

Of course, the headquarters for the Ghosts of Gettysburg tours is haunted! I was fortunate to have the opportunity to investigate this building with a small group of others. It was blazing hot that night, so I was really hoping for a few cold spots.

I was immediately drawn to what they call the Green Room, where I sensed the presence of a woman who seemed concerned about the current furnishings; in particular, she lamented the complete lack of chairs when visitors had been invited into her home. She enjoyed having visitors and entertaining.

My impressions were validated when they said that they have had experiences with a female spirit that used to live there and cares very much about her former home – Mrs. Kitzmiller.

Former hostess still receives guests at the Ghosts of Gettysburg Headquarters.

We were told that the Green Room was mainly haunted by a Confederate soldier from Louisiana named Hank. Our guide used a pendulum to attempt to communicate with him during an EVP session. The ghost communicated that he was there and that he wanted to talk. In spite of that, he did not say much other than to confirm he was from Louisiana and that he fought in the Battle of Gettysburg.

In addition, there is also a little boy named William that haunts the place and they are sometimes visited by the spirit of another little boy named Jeremy. When we began talking about the spirit called Jeremy, we began to have all kinds of spikes on EMF meters and could hear whispery responses to the questions being asked. We were told that Jeremy likes to divide his time among various buildings in the area, so you never know where you might run into him.

TRAVELER'S NOTE

271 Baltimore Street
Gettysburg, Pennsylvania 17325
www.ghostsofgettysburg.com

TILLIE PIERCE HOUSE

This historic Bed and Breakfast is right next door to the Ghosts of Gettysburg headquarters and makes a great base for exploring haunted Gettysburg. You may not even need to leave the bed and breakfast to find ghosts because they have plenty going on right there.

This inn was the private home of the Pierce family during the Battle of Gettysburg. This area of Baltimore Street saw some fierce fighting and Tillie Pierce, 15 years old at the time, was a witness to the events that unfolded around her. She later wrote a biographical account of her experiences and became known as the civilian voice of the battle. The most actively haunted room is said to be the Anna Garlach Room. At least one guest fled in the middle of the night, unable to stay there.

A paranormal group from Pennsylvania was conducting an investigation there and at around 3 a.m., they all heard a woman speaking very loudly in a foreign language. The voice was recorded as it echoed all around them. I heard the recording of it and it is absolutely bone-chilling. The language was not known to any of those present during the experience and it was not recognizable to any of us as we listened, so it remains a mystery.

In addition to voices, guests may also have their sleep disturbed at 3 a.m. by rattling or banging shutters and by phantom cannon fire.

TRAVELER'S NOTE

303 Baltimore Street
Gettysburg, Pennsylvania 17325
www.tilliepiercehouse.com

THE LITTLE DRUMMER BOY CAMPING RESORT

We stayed here during our last visit to Gettysburg without any thought as to whether it was haunted or not. The first night, we were awakened in the middle of the night by the sound of footsteps going right past our cabin. We got up to check and there was no one there. As soon as we settled back down, again we heard the footsteps. They sounded like marching and seemed to come not just from outside, but from all around us.

Exploration of Gettysburg revealed that the area where the campground is located, like much of Gettysburg and the surrounding area, was part of the battlefield. The campground is a stone's throw from Cavalry Hill and is surrounded by historical markers referring to the battle.

TRAVELER'S NOTE

1 Rocky Grove Road
Gettysburg, Pennsylvania 17325
1-800-293-2808
www.drummerboycampresort.com/

WASHINGTON, D.C.

LAFAYETTE SQUARE

Lafayette Square today is a public park and a National Historic Landmark District. Back in the eighteenth century, it was a completely different place; used as a graveyard, an orchard, a racetrack, and a market. It wasn't named Lafayette Square until 1823, when the name was changed from President's Park to Lafayette Square in honor of Lafayette's visit.

Today, there is no evidence of the graveyard or the marketplace, but the square contains some otherworldly reminders of its past inhabitants and events that make it the most haunted area in Washington, D.C.

Most people know who Francis Scott Key was. He wrote the "Star-Spangled Banner." Less well-known was Philip Barton Key, Francis' son. He was murdered in Lafayette Square by a jealous husband, Congressman Daniel Sickles. It seems that Key was having a fling with Sickles' wife. He would signal to her from the square by waving a white handkerchief.

One day, instead of his lover running to his side when he waved the handkerchief, he was confronted by her husband, pistols at the ready. Despite Key's pleas for mercy, Sickles shot him there on the square and was acquitted of all charges due to a successful temporary insanity plea.

Perhaps this is why Philip Barton Key is still seen walking the square, not in search of his love, but in search of justice.

TRAVELER'S NOTE

H Street
Between 15th and 17th Streets, N.W.
Washington, D.C. 20006

DECATUR HOUSE

Commodore Stephen Decatur moved to the new capital in 1816 and decided to live in what was going to be a very fashionable neighborhood, President's Park. Theirs was the first private residence there and they made quite a splash of it, throwing several elaborate and memorable parties.

Sadly, their happiness didn't last. Commodore Decatur had overseen the conviction of Commodore James Barron. Decatur then took over Barron's post. Barron blamed Decatur for destroying his career and challenged him to a duel. On March 22, 1820, two shots were fired at the dueling grounds in Bladensburg, Maryland . Both men were wounded, but only one was wounded fatally – Stephen Decatur. He was carried back to his beloved home and he died there in the first-floor bedroom.

His wife became overwrought and couldn't bear to live in the house. She sold off most of the furniture and moved to Georgetown, renting out the Decatur House to a series of dignitaries.

It's not clear when it was first noticed that the spirit of Stephen Decatur never left the house. Passersby reported seeing a man staring out of the window of the house, even when there was no one there. It is said that this is why several of the windows have been bricked up. This hasn't kept Stephen Decatur away, though. He has even been known to venture out into the square sometimes, carrying a box under his arm, thought to be the box containing the dueling pistols.

TRAVELER'S NOTE

1610 H Street, N.W.
Washington, D.C. 20006
202-218-4338
www.decaturhouse.org/

HAY-ADAMS HOTEL

This prestigious hotel overlooking the White House got its name from the two mansions that were demolished in order to build it – the Adams Mansion and the Hay Mansion. It seems they got rid of everything from the two old mansions except the ghost!

The ghost of Marian Hooper "Clover" Adams has been seen and heard on the fourth floor. She was an artist with an artistic temperament. She was prone to periods of depression, and during one of these, she drank some photography chemicals and committed suicide. Some people thought the behavior of her husband following her death was unusual and there were rumors that she was murdered. These rumors were never proven, however, and her husband was buried next to her.

Clover makes her presence known by opening locked doors, turning clock radios on, crying, and by occasionally hugging some of the staff.

TRAVELER'S NOTE

Sixteenth & H Streets, N.W.
Washington, D.C. 20006
202-638-6600
www.hayadams.com/

THE WHITE HOUSE

Overlooking Lafayette Square is one of the most famous buildings in the world, the White House. Ghosts have been reported throughout the entire building, from the attic to the rose garden. The most well-known ghost of the White House is probably Abraham Lincoln, who has been seen in the Lincoln Bedroom, the second-floor halls, and the Yellow Oval Room. Other presidents whose spirits have been experienced at the White House are William Henry Harrison, Andrew Jackson, Thomas Jefferson, and John Tyler.

An interesting bit of history is that many séances were held in the White House during Lincoln's time. Spiritualism was very popular, and they had lost a young son who they desperately desired contact with.

TRAVELER'S NOTE

1600 Pennsylvania Avenue, N.W.
Washington, D.C. 20500

WILLIAMSBURG, VIRGINIA

Visiting Colonial Williamsburg is like taking a trip back in time to the days before the American Revolution. The many shops, buildings, and attractions are all designed to give visitors an idea of what life was like back then. In addition to the physical sights and sounds, one may also run into some of the metaphysical or spirit residents of Williamsburg in one of the following places.

THE PUBLIC GAOL

The Public Gaol was built in 1701, mainly to provide a holding area for runaway slaves and those unfortunates who were sentenced to be branded, hanged, or whipped. During the Revolution, the inmates included Tory spies, deserters, and traitors.

Among the more colorful inmates were fifteen members of the pirate Blackbeard's crew and Henry "The Hair Buyer" Hamilton, who was placed there in 1779 because he bought pioneer scalps from Native Americans.

It is not known exactly who haunts the public gaol, but visitors have heard banging and laughing coming from one of the cells. Paranormal investigators have had unexplained malfunctions in their equipment as well as anomalous EMF readings.

TRAVELER'S NOTE

Nicholson Street
Williamsburg, Virginia 23185

THE ARMORY

This building was erected in 1715 to replace an earlier one. The Armory is set up today much as it would have been in colonial days, containing all of the supplies needed by the army. It contains everything from blankets and canteens to swords and rifles. The dangers to the community at that time were Native American raids, pirates, and slave revolts.

The Armory took its place in American history when the Gunpowder Incident took place there on the night of April 20, 1775. The governor had ordered the arsenal to be emptied and the muskets that were held there disabled. It was supposed to be a covert operation, but the soldiers were spotted by colonists, who met in the Market Square. The people who met there were intent on confronting the governor physically, but reason prevailed

Does a phantom soldier still run for his weapon in the armory?

and they sent a delegation to the governor to demand an explanation. The governor lied and this created a bigger breach in the relationship between the colonists and the English government.

It may be that echoes from that night are still heard in the old Armory. The ghost of a soldier runs up the stairs and stops at the door where the weapons and powder are held. Is this one of the governor's men who realized they had been seen and fled to their ships in the harbor? Or is it a soldier preparing for a raid or revolt? Whatever his mission, he is still determined to carry it out.

TRAVELER'S NOTE

Duke of Gloucester Street
Williamsburg, Virginia 23185

PUBLIC HOSPITAL FOR PERSONS OF INSANE AND DISORDERED MINDS

Colonial Williamsburg is also the home of the first building in North America devoted solely to the treatment of the mentally ill. The museum features two cells, each containing an iron ring on the wall, which was used to chain the patient to the wall.

The other half of the museum contains various treatment implements which were used in the early days of the hospital, when mental illnesses were thought to be brain diseases. Treatments included restraint, strong narcotics, baths in ice-cold water, and bleeding. They have replicas of various treatment devices, including a quiet chair, which was used to restrain violent patients and a long box, resembling a coffin, which was also used to restrain patients who were out of control. To the modern eye, these things more resemble torture than treatment devices.

The feeling in the cell areas was one of great sadness and confusion. The spirits there still wander, unsure about their place now that the doors are all opened and the building has been transformed into a museum, with a constant stream of visitors during operating hours. They wandered in and out of the rooms and the hallway, frightened by some of the equipment that was displayed there and uncertain about what they were supposed to do. They did not seem interested in moving on; most of them were content to just roam about between the rooms, avoiding the displays of treatment devices.

It is not clear why these souls remain in this place. Perhaps it was their home in life and they are too full of anxiety about transitioning to leave it.

TRAVELER'S NOTE

Francis Street
Williamsburg, Virginia 23185

HISTORIC POWHATEN PLANTATION

A resort in Williamsburg is crowned by this beautiful mansion. It is like an unexpected slice of history in the middle of modern luxuries. I had elected to stay at this resort because it was the only one that was located on the grounds of a former plantation and featured the plantation house and some of the outbuildings.

There have been so many paranormal experiences here that the resort has a ninety-minute ghost tour of the mansion, during which they share many of the stories associated with the place, along with the unexplained occurrences to back them up.

The plantation house that stands today is not the original house. The original house was built, in 1735, by Richard Taliaferro. When he passed away in 1779, he left the land and Powhatan Plantation to his son. During this time, the plantation was a successful venture where they raised horses, cattle, and acres of crops. After the deaths of the Taliaferros, the plantation passed through a few different owners until 1827, when it was purchased by Thomas Martin, who returned it to its original purpose as a working plantation. His son, Dr. William Martin, was the owner in 1862 when the mansion was destroyed by fire set by Union soldiers. After the Civil War, Dr. Martin rebuilt the

Powhaten Plantation's ghosts are not at all shy.

home and moved back in. After his death, it again passed through different hands until the present day, when it became the centerpiece of a resort.

Ghosts have made their presences known all throughout the house, from the basement to the third floor. The main ghost is called Eliza, who is buried in a plot on the property not far from the house. She was visiting Powhatan when she died suddenly and had to be buried in the family plot. The interesting thing is that there is only one marker in the plot, Eliza's; so where are the other family members buried? I think there must be at least a few unmarked graves on the property.

We walked into the second-floor dining room, and as we viewed various photos that had been taken during ghost tours, we saw the two doors to the hutch slowly swing open. The doors were closed, and a few minutes later, it happened again.

The lonely tombstone that was once part of a family plot.

We conducted several tests to see if we could get the doors to open by walking, stomping, closing the door, jumping, etc., but nothing would cause the them to open. Our guide told us that they believe opening the hutch doors is Eliza's way of making her presence known.

We sat on a bench in one of the upstairs rooms to hear some of the stories associated with that room. As I sat, I became very distracted by something that was pinching my behind! My daughter was on one side of me and there was a lady on the other side, neither of which had appeared to move, so I turned around to see if there was something on the bench that was pinching me. As I did, the lady sitting to my

The pinching bench.

right turned around and also began feeling around the back of the seat. I asked her, "Did you feel something pinch you?" She replied, astonished, "Yes! Did you?"

I confirmed in an excited whisper that I did feel something pinch me. Neither of us could find anything on the seat that could have caused the feeling. By this point, our whispers had been noticed by the guide who asked us what was wrong. I replied that we had both been pinched by something on the bench. She laughed and then told us that this commonly happened to women sitting on that bench! The bench was not original to the house, but had come from a church. Perhaps the bench brought a mischievous spirit with it. I cannot attribute the pinching to a lady like Eliza.

My daughter and I decided to break off from the group after the tour and go to a room to do an EVP session. We found a small room that was set up like an office, dimmed the lights, and closed the door. We looked for a lock but didn't see one, so we hoped we would have at least a few uninterrupted moments to try and make contact with the spirits there.

We began by greeting the spirits there and inviting them to talk with us. We started out with the usual questions like, "Who is here with us?" and "Would you like to tell us something?" and had progressed to asking for names and dates when we heard someone approaching. Shutting off the recorders, we waited in the near darkness for whoever it was to see the closed door and leave. Unfortunately, the footsteps came closer and were coming right up to the door. The knob began to turn and then…nothing. The knob turned the other way, shook a few times, and still stayed closed. We heard two people on the other side of the door talking about how the door must be locked. My daughter and I looked at each other and I walked over to the door and opened it with no problem, scaring the life out of the people on the other side.

They asked why we had locked the door and we informed them that we did not lock it and pointed out that there was no lock on the door. We then closed the door again from the outside and showed that it opened with no problem. We even went back inside, shut the door, and had the two people open it again with no problem.

They then asked us if we had been holding the door from the inside. We had not, and could not get the same thing to happen again with the door. When we asked the guide about the door, she informed us that, frequently, when doors are closed in the house, staff is unable to open them. She said they usually ask Eliza nicely to let them in, and then the door opens.

I felt very strongly that the ghost of the house was a lady, but was not Eliza. I felt instead that she was a lady who had lived in and presided over the house…perhaps one of the Martins or the Slaussons, who operated a dairy farm there in the early part of the twentieth century. I felt that her name was Rebecca. I was told there was a Rebecca who lived in the old house, Rebecca Cocke, who was the wife of Richard Taliaferro, Jr. They lived there with their ten children during the Revolutionary War.

Since the house was rebuilt to look exactly like the old house, and was built on the foundations of the old house, it is possible that Rebecca could still be there, watching over the place and maybe even keeping people who she feels are "interrupting" out of rooms until they ask politely to enter.

TRAVELER'S NOTE

3601 Ironbound Road
Williamsburg, Virginia 23188
757-220-1200

CEMETERIES

LAUREL HILL
PENNSYLVANIA

Do spirits walk among the beautifully carved monuments and shady pathways here? We went one night to find out. Laurel Hill is a huge ninety-five acres of massive mausoleums and monuments as well as seemingly miles of more typical grave markers.

Although it is unusual for cemeteries to be haunted, we felt this one was worth checking out since one of our members, who had visited the cemetery for historical research, returned with a photo that he felt indicated a presence near one of the monuments. He also reported feeling a very negative feeling in the area where he took the unusual photo.

One of the few cemeteries in America that is designated a Historic Landmark, many of the area's elite chose to be buried here. In fact, after the former estate became a cemetery in 1836, the proprietors set out to actively market the cemetery to the rich and famous, as being buried near people like Continental Congress secretary Charles Thomson, Declaration of Independence signer Thomas McKean, Hugh Mercer, hero of the Battle of Princeton, and George Meade, Union General at the Battle of Gettysburg was a selling point to the not-so-rich and famous.

We walked around the cemetery and identified a few areas where we felt the presence of a spirit or spirits. One of our members remarked that he felt a very negative feeling at one of the big mausoleums. It was the mausoleum of Henry Disston, the same monument where the unusual photo had been taken.

There is nothing in the life of Henry Disston that would give one cause to believe he would not be at rest. He worked very hard his entire life to build a saw-making empire and always strove to keep living conditions good for the workers in his factory. He seems to have had a strong sense of community and was, by all accounts a devout Christian. Perhaps the negative feeling was not coming from Mr. Disston, but from someone nearby.

A misty shape forms near the roof of the Disston Mausoleum.
Photo Courtesy of Rich Hickman.

Another area where the other psychic and I agreed there was a presence was the Muse monument, which is the grave of Henry Charles Lea. The caretaker concurred that he had also felt there was a presence in that area. Henry Charles Lea was a well-known historian and activist in Philadelphia who never hesitated to speak his mind about public projects. He opposed the building of City Hall at Broad and Market Streets and even organized a public demonstration in support of his alternate plan. Maybe he is there at Laurel Hill watching over things with his beloved muse of history.

An orb near the Muse Monument.

There was one other area in the cemetery where I felt as if I was being watched. Right before we left, I said out loud to the general area, "This is your last chance to show yourself. We are leaving." I think someone heard me because when I reviewed the photo later, I saw a misty shape forming in one of my photographs shot in the area.

I know that, as a rule, cemeteries are not haunted, but Laurel Hill is so much more than a cemetery. It was designed as a pleasure garden and is a real oasis in the midst of the city, where one can still find peace and beautiful views of the river below. I do not find it odd that some of the local residents may have decided to spend their afterlife in such a place.

A mist seems to be forming into a figure near graves at Laurel Hill.

TRAVELER'S NOTE

3822 Ridge Avenue
Philadelphia, Pennsylvania 19132
www.thelaurelhillcemetery.org/index.php?flash=1

TIMBUCTOO
NEW JERSEY

I ended up here by accident after making a wrong turn on the way to Mount Holly. The historical marker says that Timbuctoo was a settlement founded in 1820 by free blacks and runaway slaves, and active in the Underground Railroad. The cemetery has graves of black Civil War veterans. Although the cemetery itself is not haunted, the woods across from it are. There was a very eerie, foreboding feeling coming from those woods and I was horrified when my 2-year-old son tried to run into them. Later, I was reviewing the audio recording and realized I still had the recorder on when he was trying to run into the woods. Right before he took off, there was a whispery voice of a little girl on the recording calling, "Liam," which is my son's name.

A lonely ghost haunts the woods around Timbuctoo.

TRAVELER'S NOTE

Church Street
Timbuctoo, New Jersey 08036

MUSEUM OF MOURNING ART
PENNSYLVANIA

This museum is in the main building at Arlington Cemetery in Drexel Hill, Pennsylvania, and contains a collection of artifacts that illustrate our culture's beliefs about death and grief. There is a hearse, a cemetery gun, and several gorgeous pieces of mourning jewelry on display. The jewelry display is where I had my experience.

I was admiring the display when I heard a woman behind me say, very softly, "Hello!" I turned around and found that I was completely alone in that section. The only explanation I had for this was that many of the pieces there were so dear to the owner that one of the owners became attached to the piece. Several of the artifacts contain human hair; taken from the deceased loved one, the piece was made to memorialize. Perhaps this concrete tie with the deceased provided a focus point for the energy of the grieving survivor, a focus that has yet to fade.

TRAVELER'S NOTE

Arlington Cemetery
2900 State Road
Drexel Hill, Pennsylvania 19026
www.arlingtoncemetery.us/

WESTMINSTER CEMETERY
MARYLAND

The most haunted part of Westminster Cemetery is *under* the church and requires an appointment to see, but it is well worth it. Visitors can visit the grave of Edgar Allan Poe; the site of the annual "Poe Toast" as well as the graves of other historic figures and Revolutionary War patriots.

Some of the reported supernatural phenomena include disembodied voices, touches by invisible hands, and unexplained cold spots. The source for the haunting of the catacombs is thought to be from a number of suicides which happened here between 1890 and 1920.

Westminster Cemetery was the site of several suicides

TRAVELER'S NOTE

519 West Fayette Street
Baltimore, Maryland 21201

ROADS

DOG KENNEL ROAD
PENNSYLVANIA

The most often repeated story about Dog Kennel Road is that the spirit of a young girl is seen sitting on the third bridge where she died. I have traveled this road many times during the day and at night and have never seen anything out of the ordinary. The first time I drove down the road to the end, I saw another bridge to the left on Paxon Hollow Road, and as I crossed that bridge, I definitely felt what I can only describe as "something".

The area is very dark at night and the roads have sharp curves and steep drops, so it is a little scary to drive it and easy to see where there may have been many accidents on the road. It is also very misty and foggy at night due to the number of streams and creeks nearby.

There is definitely "something" on Dog Kennel Road.

HENSEL ROAD
PENNSYLVANIA

According to legend, an old man is seen walking up and down the road and a glowing light comes out of the woods, hovers over the road then disappears back into the woods. I guess this is a combination ghost and UFO legend. I was never able to uncover a reason for the haunting or any background information on this particular story, but there is no denying there was something going on up at Hensel Road.

This road was once a short dirt road surrounded by undeveloped land. There were rumors that a farmer had found some kids partying on his property and killed them before committing suicide.

Over the years, carloads of teenagers and other thrill seekers have driven down the road, stopping and turning off their lights to see what they could see. They would sit in the darkness of the parked cars, chatting and sometimes trying to scare each other.

Several of these people reported suddenly being aware of glowing blue lights behind and next to the cars they were sitting in. The lights would appear to hover about six to fifteen feet above the road. They are described as being about the size of a tennis ball, surrounded by a larger glowing halo. After a minute or so, the light would fade and disappear.

Don't jump into your car and head off on a search for the Hensel Road lights, though. The whole area is developed now and the place where the light once appeared is probably in someone's kitchen or family room. The approximate location now is between Route 413 (Durham Road) and Burnt House Hill Road.

I haven't heard any new reports of lights or paranormal activity in that housing development, but I have to wonder how they got the name Burnt House Hill Road. A little macabre sounding, don't you think?

LADY IN WHITE
PENNSYLVANIA

Who is the woman in white that is seen walking down Route 291 out by the Philadelphia Airport? She is said to be the ghost of a bride who was killed in a tragic accident on the way to the airport after her wedding. As they drove down 291 on the way to the airport, they were struck head on by another vehicle. Both the bride and groom were injured but alive, and the bride left her husband at the crash and walked down the road for help. When the police found the bodies the next day, they found the body of the husband and the driver from the other car. The body of the woman was half a mile down the road. In an alternate version of the story, the body of the bride was never found.

Urban legend? I thought so until I heard the following account of a personal encounter with the woman in white. A friend's brother worked in Tinicum on Governor Printz Boulevard, which is Route 291. He was leaving work at 3 a.m. one night, and in an attempt to get home quickly took a shortcut down the road that led through the marshes to the Philadelphia airport. This road is heavily traveled at night and there are lots of accidents on it. As he was driving carefully down the road, he saw a woman on the side of the road. Her head was hanging down and she was wearing all white. She was so white she seemed to glow.

He initially thought that maybe all white against the street lights on a dark night would appear to glow, even though in reality he knew she was not of this world. He slowed and tried to get a closer look. As he neared her, he realized to his horror that she was floating; her feet were above the ground. He glanced back at the road to make sure no cars were approaching and when he looked back to the woman, she was gone.

He didn't know what or whom he had seen until he told some friends about the experience and they related to him the story of the ghostly bride.

GARDEN STATE PARKWAY
NEW JERSEY

This road that runs through the whole state and is haunted by a ghost called the Parkway Phantom. He has been seen in various places, but most often near the Route 37 exit for Tom's River. The Phantom is seen at night and always in the northbound lane, waving his arms wildly as if trying to flag down passing cars. Described as tall and wearing an old-fashioned looking overcoat, he is often mistaken for a driver who needs help.

A professor at Brookdale Community College in New Jersey collected Parkway Phantom sightings and interviewed witnesses. His research concluded that the Parkway Phantom appeared about five times a year and is still reported by travelers on the Parkway.

THE OLD LADY OF SHADELAND AVENUE
PENNSYLVANIA

One day, my husband and I were traveling west on Shadeland Avenue in Drexel Hill, preparing to make a left turn onto Garrett Road towards Burmont Road. We were waiting for the light to change and making small talk when we both suddenly stopped talking and looked at each other. I am not sure who said, "Did you just see that?" first, but we nearly said it at the same time.

What we had both seen was what we thought was an old lady because of the way she was dressed. She was wearing a hat and a bulky, long, old-fashioned coat and was carrying a big old-fashioned handbag. She was dressed just like my grandmother used to dress. What was odd about her was not so much her clothing, but that as we were watching her pass by the entrance to the funeral home on the corner, she vanished.

I would have chalked this up to imagination if we both hadn't seen the same thing at the same time. We drove slowly by the funeral home, just to make sure, but it was closed and dark inside. There was no sign of the lady we had seen hurrying by.

We never saw her again after that day, but every time we were in that area, one of us would ask, "Do you remember when we saw that lady disappear?" I asked some people I know who live in the area, but no one seemed to have ever heard any reports of this. We were left wondering who and what we saw that day and hoping to see it again so we could take in more detail.

While doing some genealogical research I ran across a news article that gave me chills. The article was dated December, 1915, and the headline read, "Woman Struck by Trolley Car; Miss Mary E. Smythe, of Drexel Hill, Probably Fatally Injured." The article described an accident in which a 43-year-old woman was attempting to cross the tracks at Rosemont Avenue on her way home and was struck by the trolley as she crossed the tracks. She had been pinned under the wheels of the car and sustained what were described as:

> ...injuries which in all probability will result in her death... It was found necessary to amputate her left leg. Her condition is grave and little hope is held out for her recovery."[20]

Although she was not struck on Shadeland, the trolley tracks are in view of the intersection, and Rosemont, where it crosses the trolley tracks, is two blocks away from where the funeral home is now. When

ROADS

I read that headline, my first thought was, "That must be the lady we saw." Now I was really wondering about her odd clothing. Could we have seen this woman? I looked through death records and obituaries but was unable to find any more information about Miss Smythe. I am not sure whether we saw a ghost or maybe some residual imprint of something that happened long ago. I am not even completely convinced that who we saw *was* Miss Smythe. At the very least, it was an interesting coincidence.

ANNIE'S ROAD
NEW JERSEY

This dark road in Totowa, New Jersey—its real name Riverview Drive—is full of sudden turns and twists, and is said to be haunted by a girl named Annie. She died there the night of her prom and remains there, seemingly to exact revenge on careless drivers.

One version of the legend says that she was thrown from the car she was in and another is that she was walking on the road and was hit by a car that was traveling too quickly down the road. She appears suddenly in a white dress and is blamed for many accidents.

Adding to the spookiness is the river, which causes sudden mists to appear in the area. In addition, the road runs by Laurel Hill Cemetery, as mentioned earlier, a huge graveyard with lots of mausoleums and statues. Some of the angel statues have been vandalized as have some of the other monuments, which make it look even creepier. Legend has it that Annie was buried in one of the mausoleums there.

FIDDLER'S BRIDGE
DELAWARE

The story is romantic and intriguing with as many variations as a Mozart sonata. In one version, the Fiddler's Bridge spans Scott's Run in Middletown. Legend says that a talented, but somewhat eccentric, fiddle player used to sit on the rail and play every night. One night, he fell and was drowned. Since that time, anyone who goes to the bridge at midnight and tosses a silver coin into the water will be rewarded with a tune from the phantom fiddler.

In another version, the ghostly fiddle player is near Lewes and is the result of a prank gone wrong. It was said that back in the early 1800s, two young men were wooing the same girl. One night, one of them hid in a tree and waited for the other man to pass by. When he did, he began playing his fiddle to frighten off the would-be suitor. The prank worked, and the man fled, thinking he had run into the old fiddler's ghost. The joker did not have long to celebrate his victory, however, for he fell from the tree and broke his neck. To this day, the crazy-sounding fiddle player of the hopeful suitor can still be heard by lone passersby.

An interesting twist to the legend appears in *Delaware: A Guide to the First State.* This occurred at the Fiddler's Bridge near Middletown during a party in the late 1800s. Eager to see if the legend was true, a group of partygoers set out for the bridge at midnight. The host gave a silver coin to one of the young ladies and told her to throw it into the water. She did, and shortly after, the group heard a melancholy fiddle tune emanate from the darkness. The reaction of the guests was not recorded, but it must have been quite profound and entertaining.

Unwilling to ruin the moment, the host kept his secret to himself for some time. The secret was that he had paid a fiddle player to hide in the dark under the bridge and begin playing when the coin hit the water.

Does this mean the legend is not true? Not necessarily. The host of the party took his guests out to the bridge to reenact the legend. At that time, in the late 1800s, the legend was widely enough known that he was able to pull off the ruse. Who knows? Perhaps if one stands on the bridge at midnight and tosses in a silver coin, one might hear the haunting music of the fiddle player.

HISTORIC BUILDINGS

BALEROY
PENNSYLVANIA

Baleroy is a well-known haunted house in Philadelphia. This reputation was due in large part to the former owner, Mr. George Meade Easby, who was always very open about sharing his paranormal experiences there and opening his home for tours.

The house was built in 1911, and did not have a reputation for being haunted until the Easby family owned it, which begs the question: Was the *house* haunted or was the *family* haunted?

Meade moved into the house when he was 6. His younger brother, Steven, was 5. When they arrived at the house, the two boys immediately ran to the fountain in the courtyard. When they leaned over to look at their reflections in the water, Meade saw his own reflection, as he expected, but his brother's reflection was a skeleton. Steven died shortly after that. Meade claimed that although his brother died, he did not leave the mansion.

Some restoration workers saw Steven in an upstairs window while they were working on the fountain. One worker saw a little blond boy, and he called his coworker's attention to it. As they were looking at the boy, he just faded away. The second worker refused to come back to the house after that. The restoration worker's son was working in the basement when he heard a voice calling his name. He answered, but when he got no response, he went to see who had called him, assuming it was his father. He soon found that they were alone in the house and his father had been on the third floor. He refused to work in the basement after that.

One night when George Easby was entertaining, he and the guests heard a loud crash from the house. Upon investigation, they found that the portrait of Steven lying on the floor of the Gallery. The painting had come off the wall and flown fifteen feet. The nail was still in the wall and the wire was still intact and undamaged on the back of the portrait. Steven is not the only family member still hanging around Baleroy. Meade has also seen his uncle and his mother.

Baleroy, one of the most haunted houses in the Mid-Atlantic.

The most famous ghost of Baleroy is Amanda, who haunts a room known as "The Blue Room." She has claimed a particular chair as her own, so much so that anyone who sits in the chair dies shortly after. Amanda had appeared on the staircase to a former curator there shortly after he had sat in her chair. He then claimed that Amanda was stalking him and he felt as though he were losing his mind. He died a month later.

There is another female spirit that haunts the second floor of the house and manifests as a bluish fog, the ghost of a monk in a brown habit has been seen in the upstairs rooms, and none other than Thomas Jefferson himself has been seen walking through the downstairs. How did the house, built in 1911, become haunted by Thomas Jefferson, who died in 1826? The answer lies in the large collection of art and artifacts that Mr. Easby collected. Amanda, the monk, and Jefferson, are attached to objects they loved in life. When Mr. Easby acquired the object, the ghost came along with it.

In an article in the *Chestnut Hill Local*, Mr. Easby is quoted as saying that he believed many of the spirits there were attached to items in the house. He was told this information during one of many séances held there. If the items, including Amanda's chair, are no longer at the house, then the spirits that were attached to them would no longer be there, either. So, it is possible that Baleroy, once called the most haunted house in the area, may no longer be haunted?

Sadly, George Easby passed away in 2005 and the mansion is currently owned privately. The owners do not allow tours and wish to be left alone. It is unclear what happened to Amanda's chair or any of the other items and artwork that Easby had collected during his lifetime. I wonder if George Easby returns from time to time to check in on the home he loved so much.

I feel strongly that Mr. Easby was himself clairvoyant and that is why he was so knowledgeable about and comfortable with the ghosts that inhabited his home. It also explains why he saw the skull on his brother's face. Someone who is not as sensitive to the unseen as Mr. Easby would likely not have the same experiences at Baleroy as he did.

THE LAZARETTO
PENNSYLVANIA

One of the most frightening things in colonial days was an epidemic. It was not yet understood what caused or spread disease. Port cities like Philadelphia were particularly vulnerable to disease brought in from other countries. Quarantine of the sick had been practiced in Europe during the plagues, and this was the method of disease control used in the colonies and Early America. After the yellow fever epidemic of 1793 killed off one tenth of Philadelphia's inhabitants, they decided to move their quarantine station further away from the city.

Essington was selected as a good location for the quarantine station due to its isolation from other settled areas and its sparse population. According to Ashmead, the quarantine station called "The Lazaretto" opened in 1801. There is some evidence that it was used during construction. The term "lazaretto" is an Italian word from the mid-sixteenth century meaning "place set aside for performance of quarantine." The name Lazaretto was derived from the biblical story of Saint Lazarus, a leper resurrected by God from the dead.

The Lazaretto was the first and last stop for many immigrants.

The Essington Lazaretto then became the first, and sometimes the last, stop for immigrants entering America. The property was used in this capacity from 1800 until the late 1800s, when it was decided to relocate the quarantine station further south to Marcus Hook. The Essington Lazaretto was then leased by the Athletic Club of Philadelphia for use as a summer home. It served in this capacity until 1916, when it became the first seaplane base in the United States. By the mid-1930s, the Lazaretto was empty and the physician's house and stables were purchased by a yacht club, who still owns that property today.

Around the time the yacht club purchased that section of the Lazaretto property, interest in the site as a historic landmark began. Unfortunately, its prime waterfront location near the city and the airport threatened the existence of the remaining structures. Fortunately for us, they were preserved and remain there today, looking over a brand new fire department and banquet hall.

We visited the Lazaretto on a frigid day in January, to see if any echoes from its past could be heard. Even with the nearby fire station, homes, and air traffic, the site has an air of desolation and isolation. All that remains of the once-busy compound of eleven buildings is the main administration building, the kitchen, and the bargeman's house. As we walked around the left side of the deserted main building, we clearly heard the voice of a woman cry out and then sob. A quick check revealed that there was no one in the building and we were alone. A review of the audio recording revealed that we did not capture the voice or the sob, but what *was* there was a woman's voice admonishing us, "Get out!"

We were admonished to "Get out!" by an unseen entity near this wing of the building.

This wing and the opposite wing were once hospital wings. Was this the voice of one of the matrons or nurses, warning us to get out and avoid possible infection? Although every effort was made to avoid epidemics by examination, containment, and then fumigation at the Lazaretto, in June of 1870, there was another outbreak of yellow fever. The dead included Mrs. Eva Kugler, wife of the steward, and Mrs. Fannie Gartsell and Beth C. McGuinnes, both nurses. At that time, they believed the infection came from some rags from an infected ship that had been burned and whose fumes were carried downriver on the wind. This outbreak was one of the main reasons for the relocation of the quarantine station to Marcus Hook.

Although the operation was relocated to Marcus Hook, the cemetery remained. As part of their efforts to contain contagious disease, the Board of Health had declared that all those who died while in quarantine were to be buried on the grounds of the quarantine station. Some records from the Athletic Club indicate that they placed their baseball diamond right next to the cemetery.

A contemporary newspaper article described the scene:

> In the grounds of that place is a space of ground about 100 feet square, where are buried threescore of bodies which have long ago been forgotten, and there is no one who can recall their names. The graves are unmarked. There are a few boards standing denoting the place of the graves, but time has obliterated the names of any which were ever there... It is in the far northwestern corner of these grounds, far away from the river, and shaded by a little scrub tree, that the bodies rest.[21]

There is an area now currently fenced off that is said by local residents to be the cemetery. Are there people buried there? Some records indicate that the graves were relocated to Arlington Cemetery in Upper Darby, but Arlington has no record of the location of these relocated graves, since it was their policy not to mark anonymous or unknown burials. There is no marker at the Lazaretto property either, but the section that is in the location described by the Athletic Club is completely fenced off and inaccessible. One local woman told of how this location was originally supposed to be part of the banquet hall complex, but some bones were uncovered during the leveling of the property. It was then decided to fence off that section and leave it as a separate space. The Lazaretto Quarantine Station historical marker stands right in front of it. Rumor has it there are plans to erect a monument to those who were buried there.

The location of the burials of those who never left the Lazaretto.

A talk with one of the firemen didn't get us into the building, but did give us more to think about. When we asked how to get permission to enter, he replied, "Why would you want to go in there?" We explained that we were doing research for a book, and he nodded, adding, "Well, I can't give you permission, but you all can go up and look in the windows if you want. Just don't be surprised if you see someone looking back."

He said that he'd heard odd, inexplicable noises from the upstairs and the other rooms. When asked if it could have been animals, he just stared at us. He added that he doesn't know any animals that can turn a light switch on. Apparently, he and others have seen lights turn on inside the abandoned structure.

He then added that there was some kind of jail cell in the basement, too. My interest piqued, I remarked, "Wow, I would love to see that!" His eyes grew wider and his voice took on a very serious tone. He turned to me and said, "You don't want to go down there."

Why not?" I asked. "Are there animals in there?"

His answer was, "You just don't want to go in there."

I could see from the look on his face that even if he could take us in, there was no way he would go in with us.

A few weeks later, I was at a local shop and I saw a lady wearing a sweatshirt with the Lazaretto on it, so I remarked on it and told her that I was writing about it. She then told me that her son had been in the building and saw tunnels in the basement that went out to the river.

This was the second time my attention had been directed to the basement of the Lazaretto. That couldn't be a coincidence. I believe there is something or someone in the basement of the Lazaretto that needs discovery.

CRAVEN HALL
PENNSYLVANIA

This colonial home served as a field hospital for the wounded from the Battle of Crooked Billet, the only significant Revolutionary battle in Bucks County. General Washington had placed about 400 militiamen under the command of Brigadier General John Lacey near Hatboro, Pennsylvania, to interfere with General Howe's (the British commander) communication and foraging expeditions to the north. The name "Crooked Billet" was given to the battle because it occurred near the Crooked Billet Tavern in Hatboro. The British cavalry completely surrounded Lacey's detachment as they slept. Although the Patriots were outnumbered by a force almost twice their size, they did manage to rally and make a stand in a wooded area. Fighting continued as the patriots retreated towards the tavern. Forced to abandon their supplies and continue their retreat, they carried the wounded and dying across farm fields to Craven Hall, where they set up a field hospital.

Craven Hall is haunted by a woman in colonial clothing.

Once the British had retreated, Lacey's men returned to the field in hopes of salvaging some supplies, but what they found was a slaughter. The fallen soldiers had been bayoneted and slashed to bits. Wounded men had been covered in straw and burned alive. An investigation followed and statements were given by locals who had heard the British brag of bayoneting the militiamen after accepting their surrender and of throwing the wounded into fires of buckwheat straw.

On May 7, General Lacey, in his official report to General Armstrong, speaks of this circumstance in the following manner:

> Some of the unfortunate, who fell into the merciless hands of the British, were more cruelly and inhumanely butchered. Some were set on fire with buckwheat straw, and others had their clothes burned on their backs. Some of the surviving sufferers say they saw the enemy set fire to the wounded while yet alive, who struggled to put it out but were too weak and expired under the torture. I saw those lying in the buckwheat straw – they made a most melancholy appearance. Others I saw, who, after being wounded with a ball, had received near a dozen wounds with cutlasses and bayonets. I can find as many witnesses to the proof of the cruelties as there were people on the spot, and that was no small number who came as spectators.[22]

The battle had left eight Patriots wounded, twenty-six dead, and fifty-eight missing. A monument to those Revolutionary soldiers who died there is on Jacksonville Road, just West of the SEPTA Station.

The family burial plot behind Craven Hall is the final resting place for nine of these Patriot soldiers, as well as various Craven and Van Sant family members. One of the most interesting features of Craven Hall is the grave marker that rests inside the hearth.

In the 1970s, the family plot was vandalized and many of the markers were damaged and some were stolen. The stone reads:

> In memory of Giles Craven, who departed this life on September 8, 1778 in the 80th year of his life.

Giles' marker was stolen during the vandalism attack on the family plot. The historical society placed an ad in the local paper requesting the return of the stolen markers, and one morning, Giles' was there on the porch. They decided to keep him safe in the hearth from then on. That was enough to make me wonder if Giles might be hanging around, waiting for his grave marker to be restored. If he was there, he didn't make his presence known that day.

There is one ghost story associated with Craven Hall, which has been repeated and published in newspapers and books. The ghost is said to be that of a man in colonial dress that appears in the front window. It was speculated that he may have had something to do with the battle. I had the good fortune to not only meet this ghost at Craven Hall, but also get his photo!

An interesting little moving orb near the tombstone they keep in the fireplace.

This ghost story started when a guide, dressed in colonial clothing, was standing by the front window one day watching the traffic pass by on Newtown Road. He caught the eye of a woman as she sat at the traffic light, and as the light changed he saw a look of shock come over her face. He quickly stepped back behind the curtain because he was afraid she might have thought he was staring at her. He was the one with the shocked look when he read an article in the local newspaper the following Halloween. There was a story written up about Craven Hall that described the ghost as a man in colonial dress who was seen by a passerby.

I was relieved to hear this story because in my tour of the house I had not experienced the presence of a man in colonial dress at all. I did, however, experience the presence of a woman who appeared to be in colonial dress.

The hallway where I saw the ghostly lady of the house.

At one point during the tour, I had even asked if there was a female tour guide in costume as I believed I had caught a glimpse of her going down the hallway as we stood in the parlor. There was no other tour guide in colonial dress there that day, so I assume that I must have seen some past mistress of Craven Hall.

We continued to the upstairs section of the house, where they have a display and presentation about a local inventor, John Fitch. As we sat to listen to a presentation about the accomplishments of John Fitch, we heard a loud bang behind us. It sounded like the door slamming or someone banging on the door. I asked where the door went and our guide showed me that it went to the kitchen. My friends all had heard the bang, but the guide didn't answer us when we asked if he had heard it. He just went over and started the video. The bang sounded to me like someone was trying to say, "Well, I am not listening to this! I am going back downstairs!"

The presentation paints Fitch as an intelligent forward-thinking man who invented the first steamboat and possessed a great deal of mechanical knowledge. When I mentioned to the tour guide that I felt someone unseen had slammed the door in displeasure at the Fitch presentation, he remarked that John Fitch was not very popular among his peers because of some controversy concerning his invention. Research revealed an even more unattractive side to Fitch's history.

According to the Craven Hall Historical Society website devoted to Fitch's life and accomplishments, he had joined the New Jersey militia in 1775 and was given the task of repairing muskets. He was quite happy to do his patriotic duty until the British approached Trenton. When he was called into active service he fled to Bucks County, not returning to Trenton until General Washington had routed the Hessians there. The belongings he had left behind in Trenton during his flight to Bucks County were found to be destroyed upon his return, so he once again retreated to Bucks County. It would not be too hard to believe that the souls of the Patriots who gave their lives there fighting for our freedom would resent a monument to a deserter.

As we left the hall, I looked back and wondered who the spirits were. When I spoke to a friend of mine who used to attend meetings at Craven Hall of our visit there, he asked, "Oh, did you see Elizabeth?"

"Elizabeth?" I asked.

"Yes," he replied, "the lady that haunts the house."

I was happy to relate that I did see a woman in colonial clothing there. He assured me that she has been seen by different people over the years. He wasn't sure how she came to be known as Elizabeth, that's just what they called her.

TRAVELER'S NOTE

Street and Newtown Roads
Warminster, Pennsylvania 18974

ROCKWOOD MANSION
DELAWARE

This beautiful mansion was built in the mid-1800s as a retirement home for a wealthy merchant, Joseph Shipley. When Shipley died in the late 1800s, the property passed, after an auction, to his great-nephew, Edward Bringhurst, Jr. In 1891, he moved into Rockwood with his wife and three youngest children, one of which was Mary Bringhurst, who lived to be 100. She inherited the mansion, and when she died, it went to her niece, Nancy Hargraves, who lived there until her death in 1972. She left it to a charitable organization and it was acquired by New Castle County and run by the Friends of Rockwood. It was after the friends took it over that the unseen residents of Rockwood became public knowledge.

The mansion is haunted by former residents, including spirits that appear as children. On my first visit to Rockwood, I found the place to be overwhelmingly full of energy. The strongest impression I had was of a woman with a very long, elegant neck. She seemed to be very proud of this feature and I had a feeling that this had been her home. When I described what I was feeling to one of the volunteers, they showed me a photo of Mary Bringhurst, who did, indeed have a very long, graceful neck!

In one of the upstairs bedrooms and hallways I felt the presence of a young boy. First he was on the bed and then he ran out of the room and down the hallway. I was snapping away, trying to capture something of what I was feeling on film, when I captured the following image.

A little boy runs up and down this hallway at Rockwood.

This young boy could be the spirit of Edward Bringhurst, who came to live at the mansion, in 1891, with his sisters, Mary and Edith. Edward was born on July 4, 1884. This means he would have been about seven years old when his family moved to Rockwood. There are some photos in the book, *Romantic Rockwood*, from 1905, which are believed to be from Edward's 21st birthday, and another book, Brandywine Valley: The Informed Traveler's Guide, says that he passed away in 1939. He liked to collect antiques and some of the items that he collected are still there.

Who is the little boy that I saw in the bedroom and hallway? It could be Edward, who chose to return to his childhood home where he likely experienced much happiness.

TRAVELER'S NOTE

Guided Museum Tours Available
610 Shipley Road
Wilmington, DE 19809
302-761-4340
www2.nccde.org/rockwood/default.aspx

LEMON HILL
PENNSYLVANIA

In 1800, a man named Henry Pratt built the mansion called Lemon Hill on property he had purchased from Robert Morris. It got the name Lemon Hill because of all the lemon trees in the Morris greenhouses.

At times, visitors have reported the smell of fresh lemons, even though the trees and greenhouses are no longer there. Apparitions of those who tended the gardens have been seen as well, still lovingly tending their gardens.

A retired Philadelphia police officer reported that in the early 1990s, two city police officers who were on patrol saw a woman in white come from the direction of Lemon Hill. She crossed the road in front of them and walked down towards the river. Something about her caused them to think she was in trouble or possibly a suicide, so they called out to her. When she did not respond, they followed her to the river, where she disappeared right in front of them.

A ghostly woman was seen walking towards the river at Lemon Hill.
Photo courtesy of Rich Hickman.

TRAVELER'S NOTE

East Fairmount Park, Sedgeley, and Lemon Hill Drives
Philadelphia, Pennsylvania 19130
www.lemonhill.org/

POE HOUSE
MARYLAND

Edgar Allan Poe, famous American author, lived at this location with his grandmother, aunt, and his cousin, who became his wife, Virginia Clemm. Poe only lived there for a few years in the early 1830s and wrote several spooky stories during that time, including *MS. Found in a Bottle* and *Berenice – A Tale,* but the house is not haunted by Edgar Allan Poe. Instead, it is haunted by an old woman dressed in antebellum clothing. This could be the spirit of Elizabeth Cairnes Poe, Edgar's aunt's mother. She passed away in 1835, which is the correct period to match the clothing. In addition to seeing this woman, visitors have reported unexplained cold spots, disembodied voices, and doors and windows opening and shutting by themselves.

Today, the house is a museum and is furnished much like it would have been during Poe's residence.

TRAVELER'S NOTE

203 North Amity Street
Baltimore, Maryland 21223
www.eapoe.org/balt/poehse.htm

BURLINGTON COUNTY PRISON
NEW JERSEY

The prison was built in 1811 and has changed little since then. The cells still have, as was required during the building, a fireplace and a window. The dark and solitary cell in the middle of the upper floor of the prison was used to house the prisoners who were sentenced to death. At least eight prisoners were held in this cell until 1908, when the death penalty was suspended. Then the cell was used as a solitary confinement cell for unruly prisoners.

Today, this cell is haunted by the ghost of a man named Joseph Clough, one of the eight people executed. He had beaten his mistress to death with a table leg and was chained to the floor of Cell 5 until he was hanged in the mid-1800s. Some visitors have heard chains clanking in this cell and others have had more intense experiences.

On my first visit to the jail, I stood for a bit outside Joseph Clough's cell and tried to communicate with the heavy presence I felt there. I stood with my recorder in hand, asking benign questions like, "What is your name?" and "How old are you?" I felt like I wasn't getting anywhere, so I said, "This is your last chance to say something to me," and next thing I knew, something smacked against my hand and the recorder flew up in the air and then hit the floor. The back came off and the batteries rolled across the floor. Figuring that my first impression that he was not in the mood to talk was right on target, I decided to gather up the pieces and head back downstairs. When I reviewed the recording later, I heard a man's deep voice. I asked the question, "Were you sentenced to death?" and the voice replied, "Yes."

It must have been the ghost of Joseph Clough or one of the other men who spent their last hours there.

Someone did not want to be recorded near this Death Row cell.

TRAVELER'S NOTE

Corner of High and Grant Streets
Mount Holly, New Jersey
www.prisonmuseum.net/

WOODBURY FRIENDS MEETING HOUSE
NEW JERSEY

The Woodbury Friends Meeting House was built in two sections, one in 1715, one in 1785. During the Battle of Red Bank in nearby National Park, the meeting house was used as a hospital by the Hessians. The Friends cemetery is on the left side of the Meeting House and runs from the bank of the creek right up to the wall of the Meeting House. Maybe even under it. The present cemetery was dug on top of the old cemetery.

When they were digging for the road that runs in front of the Meeting House, a place was needed to put the dirt. The Friends offered to let some of the fill be placed on top of the old cemetery. They then proceeded to bury people in that ground. The result is a two-level cemetery, with the current one directly on top of the older one.

What is not mentioned in most history books is that there was an even older burial ground there. A marker in the middle of the cemetery tells some of the story.

It was originally used as a burial ground by the Indians... This monument and the remains of twenty-one known and a number of unknown persons [The Indians?] interred in the Wood Burial ground near the mouth of the Woodbury Creek were removed to this site March 9, 1951 in accordance with the judgment of the Superior Court.

What had happened was that some of the remains from the older burial ground were washed away into the creek during a very bad storm. What to do with those remains was decided by a court order. The remains were interred in the meeting house burial ground in a common area.

So who haunts the Meeting House? Is it a Hessian soldier or is it one of the people whose resting place was disturbed and displaced? Perhaps it is just someone who decided to stay at the meeting house.

One of the Friends reported that there is one particular seat that is always avoided by the Friends during their meetings. Every time someone has sat in that seat, they have become uncharacteristically angry and argumentative.

They had tried several times and even tried different methods for cleansing or clearing the spot. Sometimes it worked for a while, but the presence would always return to that same corner. It is not known whose presence was the source of the discomfort, but I felt it had something to do with a burial spot.

When we went outside, I noticed that the markers ran right up to the edge of the meeting house. I felt as if there were other burials that were now *under* the meeting house and the feelings of anger were emanating from that area.

The argumentative corner at the Meeting House.

TRAVELER'S NOTE

124 N. Broad Street
Woodbury, New Jersey 08096

GRUMBLETHORPE
PENNSYLVANIA

This was once the summer home of the Wister family. The house became their primary residence during the yellow fever epidemic. The family was not in residence during the Battle of Germantown and British General James Agnew chose the house for his headquarters. The general was fatally wounded in the battle and died in the front parlor, where his blood stains can still be seen on the floor. But his bloodstains are not the only thing that lingers at the house. The General's ethereal presence can be felt there as well. And it goes further because the General's ghost is not the only presence at Grumblethorpe. The other spirit is said to be that of a woman named Justinia. She was orphaned in the yellow fever epidemic and taken in by the Wisters. Justinia loved to bake bread, and baked every Friday night for distribution to the poor on Saturday morning. Justinia died in 1820, but her spirit has never left the house that was her home. Sometimes her presence is accompanied by the sweet smell of freshly baked bread.

According to an article by Rick Fink, not long ago, the caretakers saw what they described as a misty white woman in colonial clothing walking in the garden. Justinia was said to have loved the garden and spent a lot of time there while in service to the Wisters.

The house is now restored and has been refurnished to match the original period, and contains many interesting pieces. Many of the things on display in the house belonged to the Wister family, like scientific equipment, Owen Wister's desk, and Sally Wister's bedroom.

Author Note: I have had the chance to investigate since I wrote this story. New information has come to light. What appears to be a bloodstain is on the floor. It is not actually a bloodstain, but a stain from the lye used to clean up the blood.

The night that we investigated here, we felt the presence of a woman in Sally's bedroom. A motion sensor placed in the bedroom kept going off when there was no one there. We also recorded two unexplained voices; one said "I don't know," and the other was a noise that sounded like a cough right after the motion sensor went off.

TRAVELER'S NOTE

5267 Germantown Avenue
Philadelphia, Pennsylvania 19144

WALNUT STREET THEATRE
PENNSYLVANIA

This is the oldest theatre in America, and the only theater continuously operating as such since its opening in 1809. According to the Walnut Street Theatre's website:

Every noteworthy American actor of the nineteenth century and many from the twentieth century appeared on stage at the Walnut Street Theatre.[23]

I first became aware of the ghost there when I was a volunteer usher. Every time I was assigned to the second floor, I would see a little girl dressed in old-fashioned clothing appear near the stairs. When I asked one of the staff, they confirmed that the theatre was haunted by a little girl. No one seems to know who she is or why she remains there.

They also told me another creepy story about the theatre. The skull used as Yorick's skull in Hamlet is a real skull! A stage hand, John "Pop" Reed had requested in his will that his head be removed from his body, cleaned to the bone, and used as Yorick's skull whenever Hamlet is performed. They complied with his wishes, but Hamlet has not been performed there lately. The skull is kept at the theatre and is signed by some of the actors who were in the play at the Walnut.

TRAVELER'S NOTE

825 Walnut Street
Philadelphia, Pennsylvania 19107
www.walnutstreettheatre.org/

MASSEY HOUSE
PENNSYLVANIA

A tribute to the American dream, this house was the home of once-indentured servant, Thomas Massey. The original section was built by Thomas in 1696 and added onto by his son, Mordecai, in 1731. Thomas died when Mordecai was only 13 years old; his youngest daughter was not even a year old. His wife, Phebe, was left with seven small children to raise. She solved this problem by marrying a widower with two children of his own.

Today, the house is open for tours and colonial dinners. Some of the visitors have experienced a brush with the supernatural when they visit to hear about the Masseys or partake of a colonial feast cooked in the hearth.

Massey House is still inhabited by the original residents.

One spirit that was seen by a volunteer's daughter was a Revolutionary War soldier that ran from the basement as she entered it. This was odd, as the Masseys and their descendants were Quakers and they did not fight in wars. History tells us, however, that Joshua Lawrence, who was born in the Massey House, did fight in the Revolution.

When I got the opportunity to investigate the Massey House, I was expecting to run into the soldier in the basement. I am glad to report that he was there, along with some other spirits!

In the upstairs bedroom, we encountered a woman in colonial dress who seemed to be very ill. I decided the best way to communicate with her would be with a "ghost box" (a radio that has been modified to receive communication from spirits). My fellow investigator, Lori Clark, and I gathered around the radio and began asking questions. We were amazed that not only did we get immediate responses, but they were very clear. To "What is your name?" we got the answer, "Phebe." We asked why she was there and the reply was, "I'm happy."

We also kept receiving the word "Pigs" over and over again. We had no idea what that meant and almost didn't mention it to Rich Paul, (official title) of the Massey House, but we were glad we asked before we left if the word had any significance. He informed us that at one time in the 1800s, the property was known as The Pig Farm!

We have been fortunate enough to make many visits to the Massey House, during which we have experienced knocks on the windows and have encountered the spirits of Phebe, the soldier, and also the spirit of a little girl who enjoyed playing with our equipment.

It was during our communication with the little girl, when we asked that she allow us to take her picture, that we captured images of her.

During a later ghost box session, we kept getting the word "Lenape" and "Lenape women." Although the entire area was once inhabited by the Lenape, we were not sure what possible connection this could have to the Massey House. Rich Paul had an idea when we asked him about it. He stated that there had been some Lenape graves right up the road from the house. Could this be the Lenape women?

In 1941, the skull of a young Okehocking female was found in a rock shelter behind Langford Road in Broomall. It was thought that she had been sleeping there when the rocks fell, killing her. Her tribe members apparently had removed the part of her body they could reach for burial elsewhere. Even more amazing was the discovery of a complete Okehocking woman found, in 1943, under another rock shelter closer to Langford Road. Someone may have been trying to tell us about these women whose burial places had been disturbed.

A shadowy spot forms in an upstairs room. *Photo courtesy of Michael Meehan*.

The shadowy spot moves across the room. *Photo courtesy of Michael Meehan*.

TRAVELER'S NOTE

Lawrence Road at Springhouse Road
Broomall, Pennsylvania 19008
www.thomasmasseyhouse.org/

MOUNT WASHINGTON TAVERN
PENNSYLVANIA

In Farmington, right up the hill from Fort Necessity, you will find this colonial inn and tavern museum. Its prime location on the National Road made it a popular stop for many years. Judging from the crowds that passed through the day I visited, it remains so today.

It was built about 1828, and was a busy place until about 1855, when traffic on the National Road lessened as railway travel increased and the tavern was purchased by Godfrey Fazenbaker. During its heyday, the tavern was run by James and Rebecca Sampey, who were instrumental in its success. "The place was clean, the food was good, the landlady was civil, and her husband was sober,"[24] which was at that time, the formula needed to run a quality establishment. Mr. Fazenbaker lived there for over three quarters of a century and kept the inn open, offering hospitality to the travelers who still occasionally passed by.

The ground floor is still divided into sections the way it would have been in the early 1800s. The parlor is large and very nicely decorated. This is the section that catered to ladies, children, and gentlemen.

The barroom was frequented primarily by men and perhaps by ladies with tarnished reputations. Although these areas and the social history of the nineteenth century were fascinating, it was not this area that drew my attention.

As soon as we entered the kitchen, I knew there was a presence there. It was a light and subtle one – unobtrusive, but very much there. It seemed to be a woman in a long, straight dress and apron. She was standing right in front of the large hearth, walking back and forth as if she were checking on various things she had cooking there. I was so focused on the ghostly woman at the hearth that I did not hear one word of what the guide said, and it was only when a second tour group came in that I realized my tour had left.

I was not sure who she was, but the woman at the hearth certainly seemed intent on watching over things. Could it have been Rebecca Sampey? The tavern was renowned for its good food and cleanliness. The food would have been cooked in large quantities in this open hearth and would have needed constant tending during busy hours. Whoever she was, I hoped she enjoyed her work. I know I would have liked to be able to kick back on one of the benches once in a while now that there were no more guests in the Tavern.

The bedrooms upstairs were surprisingly large, I thought. Then I saw that the rooms were communal. If you stayed at the inn you would sleep with strangers! There was one room that seemed to have a lingering guest from the past.

There were a number of people walking in and out, but I was able to have about 20 minutes up there alone to try and make a connection with the spirits of the Tavern. The first thing I heard was the babbling of a young baby. Looking around, I saw that there was no one else on the second floor with me. Given the communal nature of the rooms, I wondered if the cradle was part of the inn furniture or if it had been from the family or possibly donated.

It seemed sad to think of a baby's ghost lingering there, untended for centuries, but the baby was babbling and gurgling and did not sound unhappy. Of the many photos I took of the room, only one of them showed anything unusual.

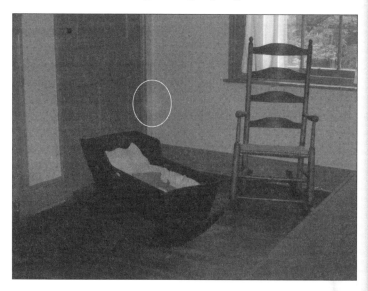

At first I thought that maybe this had something to do with the baby's spirit. On reflection, however, I thought maybe the orb of light was what the baby ghost was gurgling and babbling at!

Others who have visited the

An orb hovers over the cradle at the Mount Washington Tavern.

Mount Washington Tavern have reported unusual photos of the cradle, as well as the spirit presence of a woman near the hearth. Some people have even encountered a ghostly bartender!

TRAVELER'S NOTE

Located off the National Road
U.S. 40, in Farmington, Pennsylvania 15437
Part of the Fort Necessity National Battlefield Park

141

THE GHOSTHUNTER STORE
NEW JERSEY

How fitting that a place that sells ghost-hunting equipment should be haunted. When Dave Juliano of South Jersey Ghost Research first opened his business here, he knew they would be sharing the building with a few unseen tenants.

Not much is known of the history of the building itself. It was a private home but is now part of the Mill Race Shops on Church Street. About thirty years ago, it was the home of a minister. The house was purchased from an elderly woman – it's not clear whether she was related to the minister's family or whether she had bought it from them – after she was pushed down the basement stairs.

The Ghost Hunter Store has several unseen residents.

A recent incident near the basement stairs involved a shield that is currently hanging over the basement door. On that day, it was business as usual in the shop when the shield, nail and all, was pulled out of the wall and landed on the floor. The basement, like the third floor, is an area that no one is comfortable in. My impression was that someone had died and their body had been held down there until it could be buried. Someone in the house went down there repeatedly to grieve over the corpse, which likely resulted in a buildup of negative energy. The feeling upon entering the basement is that you are intruding – maybe interrupting the grieving person?

The shop itself is haunted by a woman. Research has not revealed the identity of this lady yet. She seems to approve of the business they have there because if visitors make fun of the shop she has been known to throw little flashlights from one of the displays at them. One day, an entire spin rack was thrown at one of the investigators with South Jersey Ghost Research who had been having a bad day. Other events credited to the mysterious woman are the unexplained chiming of the doorbell and the sink in the showroom coming on full blast all by itself.

Upstairs is a heavier, less playful presence. He makes himself known by rattling the door to the third floor and has been known to open the door on occasion. Recently, he smashed a fire alarm that had been hanging above the third-floor door. He seems very territorial about this area, to the point where no one is comfortable going up there.

The impression that I had during our visit to the third floor was that a mentally ill woman was kept there by this man. She was suffering from a severe depression or something similar and was kept locked in the front room. The whole scene was very reminiscent of *The Yellow Wallpaper* by Charlotte Perkins Gilman. Dave Juliano said that several visiting psychics have reported the same scene.

Marti, a psychic who works in the shop and teaches classes there, said that, at times, the energy they associate with the man can be overwhelming. This is especially true towards the end of October, when everyone who works in the shop seems to get short with each other. Who the man is and why he remains there is a mystery, but what he looks like is not. One night, Marti took a shower as she was preparing to teach a class that night. As she opened the curtain she was face to face with a rough-looking man, tanned with dark, wavy hair. She described this as the most disturbing experience she has had in the building. Was he a former resident who perhaps disapproves of the current use of the place? So far, he has remained silent on the subject.

Another possible source of the haunting in the shop is the Battle of Iron Works Hill, also known as the Battle of Mount Holly, a small series of skirmishes that kept the Hessians and British under Von Donop from being in a position to assist the night Washington crossed the Delaware. Because of the skirmishes, it is possible that a few soldiers from that engagement remain in the area.

Visits to the shop are always interesting and the staff is happy to discuss the experiences they have had there. You may even have an experience of your own; I know that I have had several brushes with the resident ghosts. Last time I was there, I was standing by the register, talking to Marti when a voice said, right in my ear, "When are you leaving?" We laughed about that and Marti said things like that are daily occurrences. I left shortly after, but I know I will be back to this place.

TRAVELER'S NOTE

16 Church Street
Mount Holly, New Jersey 08060
609-261-2361
www.ghosthunterstore.com

SCHOOLS AND UNIVERSITIES

WILKES UNIVERSITY
PENNSYLVANIA

Reports of paranormal activity at Wilkes University come from many of the buildings, most of which are converted nineteenth-century mansions.

WECKESSER HALL

If you are looking for a haunted building on campus, chances are you will be directed to Weckesser Hall. It was once the grand castle-like home of a former director of the F.W. Woolworth Company and much of the opulence of that mansion has been retained, including an elevator, a surround shower, and a huge chandelier.

When John Zaffis, renowned demonologist and ghost hunter, lectured at Wilkes in 2009, he investigated Weckesser Hall with some students, many of whom felt that they received confirmation of a haunting that had just been a rumor until that night. The most common occurrence reported here is a shadowy form that descends the main staircase and moves towards the front of the house.

KIRBY HALL

Kirby Hall is currently the home of the humanities department, and there seems to be a presence on the third floor. Unexplained footsteps echo from the staircase and some security guards have even felt a ghostly but supportive hand on their backs as they patrol the halls here.

It was a private home until 1941, when it was given to the University by Allen P. Kirby. In 1943, the third floor was converted to be the living quarters of the first University president, Dr. and Mrs. Eugene Farley, who moved here from Weckesser Hall to make room for a military training program. Before long, expansion of the library took over the third floor as well, and the Farleys moved again. Is it one of the Farleys who walks the halls of Kirby at night or is it a former student or professor doing some late night research in the former library?

STURDEVANT HALL

In 1940, Wilkes purchased the building known as Sturdevant Hall. It was used for off-campus events, a girl's dormitory, administration offices, and a co-ed dormitory. Through all these changes, the reported experiences were constant. There would be a knock on a closed door. The occupant would get up to answer it, only to find there was no one there.

TRAVELER'S NOTE

84 West South Street
Wilkes-Barre, Pennsylvania 18766
www.wilkes.edu

BLOOMSBURG UNIVERSITY
PENNSYLVANIA

PHI SIGMA SIGMA HOUSE

There are a few different haunted buildings around this campus. One is the Phi Sigma Sigma House, said to be haunted by a lady who moves objects, opens and closes doors, and turns the television on.

She has tapped people on the shoulder, and disconcertingly pushed someone down the stairs. How do they know it is a lady? Some of the sisters have woken up in the middle of the night to see a woman standing at the foot of the bed looking down at them. Alarmingly, one sister woke up in the middle of the night feeling as if she were pinned to the bed, being choked. Sisters have also complained about extreme drafts of coldness and one sister has even seen a shadowy figure standing near her radiator. According to research done by the tenants, a woman fell to her death on the stairs in the early 1900s, and it is believed to be her spirit that haunts the house.

TRAVELER'S NOTE

323 Lighthouse Street
Bloomsburg, Pennsylvania 17815

BLOOMSBURG RESIDENCE HALLS

COLUMBIA HALL

This residence hall is said to be haunted by two spirits, one is that of a girl who was murdered by her boyfriend. The room where this supposedly happened is marked by cold drafts and occasional disembodied screams.

A second ghost haunts one of the bathrooms and is said to be that of a girl who committed suicide by hanging herself in the shower. She lets residents know she is there by turning hair dryers on and off and by making an alarm clock go off repeatedly.

TRAVELER'S NOTE

www.bloomu.edu/

ANOTHER HOUSE ON LIGHTHOUSE STREET

Moving into off-campus housing at Bloomsburg University doesn't guarantee you will be unhaunted as one group of girls found out. It started when the landlord asked them if they were afraid of ghosts. They were not, so they moved in.

They think the ghost is an old woman who had the house built in 1932 and lived there for her entire life. She never married nor had children. After her death, the house stood vacant for quite a while until it was purchased for housing for students.

The ghost makes her presence known by opening doors and walking up the squeaky old staircase. They have also heard footsteps in the attic, which is locked by the landlord, so the tenants have never been up there.

So are they afraid of ghosts now? The tenants admit to not wanting to go downstairs alone to check on laundry, but mostly they feel as if the spirit there is protective and benevolent.

DREW UNIVERSITY
NEW JERSEY

Mead Hall once was Drew University, started in 1867 by Daniel Drew. He named the building Mead Hall in honor of his wife, Roxanna Mead Drew. Before the Drews purchased it, it was known as "The Forest" and was a private home for William Gibbons, his wife, four children, and the staff of servants a home of this size required.

The mansion was built in 1836 and the Gibbons family resided there for only eight years before Mrs. Gibbons passed away. Mr. Gibbons died suddenly of a heart attack in 1852. The house was left to William Heyward, the Gibbons' only son, who lived in Savannah, Georgia. It stood vacant for fifteen years when William Heyward, who had lost everything due to his support of the Confederacy during the Civil War, sold the house to Daniel Drew. Drew wasted no time in starting his seminary school.

Sadly, in 1989, the building caught fire and was damaged extensively. It has since been restored and owes its continued success to the dedicated people at the University as well as the Friends group that exists to ensure the preservation of this building. During the fire, it is said that firemen saw a woman in old-fashioned clothing walking through the flames. The ghostly woman of Mead Hall is traditionally thought to be Roxanna Mead Drew, the building's namesake, but I think it is far more likely that it is the ghost of Mrs. Gibbons, who didn't get to enjoy her beautiful home very long.

TRAVELER'S NOTE

36 Madison Avenue
Madison, New Jersey 07940
www.drew.edu/

COMMUNITY COLLEGE
PENNSYLVANIA

This campus used to be an Agricultural and Industrial School for inner city youth. I became acquainted with the spirits here while teaching a Paranormal Investigation class. A security guard reported that employees felt uncomfortable in the gym area and did not like to go there alone. It was a perfect set up for the class to be able to test out their new skills! The gym is one of the remaining original buildings from the Agricultural and Industrial School. The adjacent classrooms were the metal shop classroom.

The first time we investigated the gym, I was drawn to the equipment closet and felt strongly that someone had committed suicide there. We recorded several EVPs, including two separate ones recorded at the same time that said, "I killed him." Research revealed both a suicide and a murder in that area, sometime in the 1950s.

In the girl's locker room, we all felt a strong presence, so we decided to do an EVP session and try to get whoever was there to communicate with us. We asked who was there and heard growling. I took a photo, which was followed by a loud bang and then more growling. One of the growls was right by my ear and could be heard on the recording.

In the gym, the security guards have seen chairs move and heard unexplained voices and noises. We were able to record many unexplained noises from the gym. During the writing of this book, I was in contact with the security guard, who reported moving chairs and unexplained noises were continuing; in fact, at one point, there was an incident nearly every day.

A moving orb in the gym at Chester County Campus.

TRAVELER'S NOTE

Chester County, Pennsylvania

THE GEORGE SCHOOL
PENNSYLVANIA

This is a prestigious academy located in Bucks County. The campus is beautiful and the school has an excellent academic reputation. It also has a reputation for being haunted, as well as having the distinguished honor of association with one of the more grisly legends in the area.

THE TATE HOUSE

The Tate House is part of the campus and houses some of the teaching staff. It was built in 1756 by Anthony Tate. His son, Dr. James Tate, inherited the house in 1781. During the Revolutionary War, Dr. James Tate acquired the body of a Hessian soldier who had died in battle. Tate carried the dead soldier to his laboratory where he dissected the body. Afterwards, he buried the remains in a shallow grave dug into the floor of his basement. This deed is the source of impenetrable darkness in the basement of the Tate house.

Legend has it that to this day, every time one walks over the grave with a lighted candle, the flame will blow out. Former owners have told of not being able to keep the pilot light of water heaters lit. If one walks over it with a flashlight, the light will go off. When the person is standing in the dark, they hear footsteps run up the stairs and across the hallway to the front door, as if trying to escape. As if that weren't enough, some residents of Tate House have actually seen the ghostly Hessian soldier standing in their bedrooms.

Are the remains still there, under the floor? This was the one question I had about the whole thing. If so, it seems that an easy solution for this haunting would be to give the bones a proper burial. If the bones have been properly buried, then it is likely the situation could be cleared up with a good cleansing of the area to remove the negative energy left by Dr. Tate's dissection.

TRAVELER'S NOTE

1690 Newtown Langhorne Road
Newtown, Pennsylvania 18940
www.georgeschool.org/

HOTELS AND RESTAURANTS

INN PHILADELPHIA
PENNSYLVANIA

Camac Street is one of the oldest streets in Philadelphia, and it is the only wooden block street in America. The wooden blocks are now under the paving. There is a tunnel under the street which may have been used in the Underground Railroad, or may have served a less noble purpose. The area has had a very interesting history. The site itself was built in 1824. For a while, Camac Street was the center of a red light district in Philadelphia. Fortunately, the area was cleaned up and it has become a very exclusive area today.

The Inn Philadelphia is really two row homes that were restored by the current owners after a fire. Staff and patrons have reported chandeliers swinging in a circle, doors mysteriously opening, a figure on the second-floor landing, and disembodied footsteps. The footsteps are described as a step/drag kind of sound. A picture in the second-floor corridor reportedly flew off the wall and hit the opposite wall. Dishes have flown off of racks in the kitchen and disembodied voices have been heard.

The footsteps may be the spirit of a previous owner's father, who had helped in the rebuilding. He became very attached to the property, and unfortunately, passed away right before his son's restaurant opened there. He was described as wearing heavy boots and walking with a limp!

The upstairs (restaurant) is said to be the most actively haunted area, with most of the activity taking place in the hallway and in the ladies room and the dining room. Two staff members reported seeing and sensing what they believe was the spirit of a woman passing by them in the upstairs hallway. They reported a swishing sound, such as that of a long skirt.

The basement of the restaurant has also been the scene of activity. It is said that it had been used as a passageway on the Underground Railroad. I am acquainted with some of the business owners on Spruce Street and they have reported that it is rumored that the connecting basements under Spruce Street and the adjoining streets, like Camac Street, were ideal for this purpose and were used for the transportation of slaves to Canada.

The business owners to whom I have spoken report similar occurrences in the basements of their buildings – like footsteps, things being moved inexplicably, and things disappearing only to reappear later in a different place in the building. Many of these businesses are being purchased now for conversion to condominiums. It will be interesting to see what gets stirred up during the construction and if the new residents of the condos experience any activity!

TRAVELER'S NOTE

251 S. Camac Street
Philadelphia, Pennsylvania 19107

MOSHULU
PENNSYLVANIA

This is the world's largest and oldest four-masted sailing ship still afloat! It was originally named *Kurt* by the German owners, and was launched in 1904 in Scotland. During World War I, she was captured by the U.S. and renamed *Moshulu*, which is Senecan for "fearless."

The Moshulu Restuarant.

The *Moshulu* has had a long, eventful history. Twenty-eight people have died on board. This ship and restaurant is haunted by the "Lantern Ghost." There are lanterns on all the tables. They are extinguished at closing time. This is always carefully checked by the employees, as the interior of the restaurant was destroyed in 1989 by a fire. Nevertheless, lanterns are found burning when the staff opens in the morning.

I recently visited the *Moshulu* to check out the lantern lighting ghost. Dinner passed without incident, so we did some exploring of the decks. It was quiet, but there was that unmistakable presence near the stairs, which seemed to follow me to the upper deck. The feeling was a strong feeling of someone not wanting me there. It was so strong I had to go back down the stairs. This felt like a different presence from the traditional lantern lighting ghost of the *Moshulu.* I felt that this was a sailor who still bristled at the presence of women on the upper deck of "his" ship.

TRAVELER'S NOTE

401 South Columbus Boulevard
Philadelphia, Pennsylvania 19106
www.moshulu.com

JARRETTOWN INN
PENNSYLVANIA

I first visited the Inn as part of a group that accompanied a local radio station as they visited various haunted locations throughout southeastern Pennsylvania. Although there was quite a crowd there, I did manage to break away at the start of the evening and set up by myself in a room on the second floor. I took some temperature readings and began to see a steady drop in the temperature towards the fireplace area. When it dropped to 12 degrees lower than the average temperature, I decided to take some photos.

I made sure to ask if the fireplace was a working one, thinking that may have accounted for the temperature fluctuation. The hostess told us that, as far as she knew, the fireplace was closed up. I returned to the room and took some readings again. This time there was no fluctuation; even by the hearth, the temperature was steady.

I was trying to figure out what was drawing me to this room. The urge to walk to the window and look out took my attention from the fireplace. The view out the window was over the back parking lot and a large stable building. The stable looked like a good place, so I headed down the stairs and out the back door.

As I headed out, I was noticed by a group of people. They must have thought I knew something – maybe my bag of ghost gear gave it away – so they all followed me. I was annoyed at the time, but in a few minutes I was really, really glad they were all there with me.

The stable doors were all locked with big, heavy padlocks. We walked over to one of the doors and someone said, "I wish we could go in there..." Their voice trailed off as we all saw the padlock lift up by itself, pull apart and then fall back against the door, unlocked.

Viewing this as an invitation, I opened the door and a few of us went inside. There was someone in there. We looked at each other and then up as our eyes followed the sound of heavy footsteps on the upper floor of the stable.

I asked aloud, "Is there someone upstairs?"

A voice answered me from outside.

"There is no one in there. In fact, there is no way to get upstairs in there. You have to get a ladder and climb up." One of the employees had followed in the group.

Although I said goodbye to the inn that night feeling very happy to have witnessed something incredible, the inn wasn't ready to say good night to me yet.

It was late when I got home and I had class the next morning, so I was hoping to fall asleep quickly. With a sigh, I pulled up the blankets and got comfortable. I heard someone crying and jumped right up.

First, I looked over at my youngest daughter, who was sleeping in bed with me. She was sound asleep. Was it imagination? I looked around the room. The windows were closed, my youngest was quiet,

This area of the Jarrettstown Inn was marked by unexplained temperature fluctuations.

and I wasn't hearing anything now. I went back to bed.

There it was again!

I glanced over at my youngest, who was still quiet. Thinking it was one of her sisters or maybe the cat, I got out of bed and resigned myself to checking the house. Walking down the dark, silent stairs, I realized quickly that the crying had stopped again. Still, I checked on my older daughters and looked out the windows. Everything was still and quiet except me!

I went back to bed and there it was again! This time, I decided to try and ignore the sobbing. Eventually, I just covered my ears, and thought to myself, "Well, whoever you are, you are just going to have to cry. I need some sleep!" I was so tired I never thought of recording it, which I am still kicking myself about.

The next morning I got up, not even thinking about the crying. I woke my daughter up and she looked at me and said, "Mommy, I couldn't sleep good last night. There was a lady in here and she kept crying." Chills covered my arms and ran up my neck, but I managed to ask her, "What did she look like?"

"Like Barbie," she replied, "with long blonde hair."

I called the Inn, thinking this would be of interest to them. They informed me that there was a tradition of a ghost on the second floor that was described as a woman who looks out the windows and cries! I haven't heard her at my house since then, so my guess is that she is back at the Inn. I value my night's sleep, so they are welcome to her.

Another interesting story came to me from someone who asked me if I had ever been to the Inn and if it was haunted. When I related the above experiences, she asked me if I knew about the tornado.

"No," I answered.

She then informed me that on May 28, 1896, a series of tornadoes tore across southeastern Pennsylvania, including the area of Jarrettown. As a result, the barn and stable were destroyed. Some servants had been in there and were killed; several others were injured. One of the unfortunate souls killed was her ancestor. She sent me a copy of the article about the tornado and the damage it caused. Are these spirits killed by the tornado the ones who play with the locks and are they the source of the disembodied footsteps?

I returned to the Inn a few more times, but the woman never appeared in my bedroom again. On these subsequent visits, I was able to talk with the staff more about the spirits there.

One night the owner even came out and shared some experiences with us. There were three things that had convinced him the place was haunted. The first time he got a chill from the place was when he was driving by one night and happened to glance over at the restaurant. He saw the shadow outline of a person standing at the window looking out towards him. He knew there was no way someone could be in there because he had set the alarm. As he was watching, the shadow just disappeared. When he went into the restaurant, the alarm was still armed and there was no sign that anyone had been there.

The next thing was really strange. He was walking around the outside of the building, just checking things, when something fell down from the roof right in front of him. He picked it up and saw that it was a plate that was dated 1897. He could not think of anything significant in the history of the place in that year, other than the tornado had hit the year before, in 1896.

The other odd thing was that every time they were cleaning up after parties late at night, he would hear a sound from the downstairs lobby area that sounded like the shrill ring of an old-fashioned telephone. There was no telephone in the place that sounded like that. He described it as a real bell sound; just like an old phone. The employees nodded in agreement. They had all heard it, too.

They also reported that from time to time when they were cleaning up at night, pint glasses from the bar would rattle and fall down inexplicably.

At one time, the third floor had been an apartment. The tenants complained of loud music late at night after closing. When they moved out, the owner asked a psychic to go through the whole building. She started up the stairs to the third floor and refused to go further. They never found out what was up there, but everyone agreed that the third floor was not a place they would go alone.

The only tragedy in the history was the tornado that killed two people in 1896. It is possible that the spirits there linger because of some yet undiscovered tragedies in the Inn's history of the building or the property.

The Jarrettown Inn is now called the Jarrettown Hotel and is an Italian Bistro, still serving great food and offering hospitality to guests, both seen and unseen.

TRAVELER'S NOTE

1425 Limekiln Pike
Dresher, Pennsylvania 19025
www.jarrettownrestaurant.com/

THE BRICK HOTEL
PENNSYLVANIA

I found the Brick Hotel as I was driving by one evening on my way home from New Hope. As I passed it, I couldn't help but be distracted by the energy of the place. I really wanted to go in there and have a look around, as I could feel from the street that the place was full of spirit energy.

That night I e-mailed the hotel, asking for permission to come and investigate. They responded very quickly with an enthusiastic, "Yes!" The employees and owner felt the same thing that I did; the place was just full of energy.

The current owner reported a recent incident when she returned one night to retrieve some forgotten money. As she entered, she saw that somehow all of the lights downstairs had been turned on again. She also had the overwhelming feeling that she had interrupted someone or something.

When I arrived at the hotel, I decided to start my visit at the bottom, in the basement, which was the area where the lights had been turned on inexplicably. There were old fireplaces and an old cooking area. I felt that there had been a different way out in the back of the basement, with soldiers coming and going through the area.

In the middle part of the basement we felt that there was some kind of connection with the Underground Railroad as we picked up on the presence of several African-American spirits grouped together. We also felt that someone had died and was buried under the basement floor. All of these impressions were met with nods from the staff. They too had felt that these things had happened here.

It wasn't clear who had turned on the lights that night, but I felt the presence of a woman grow stronger as we walked back towards the stairs and towards the women's bathroom. As we headed upstairs, the presence was even stronger and was joined by several other presences. This hotel was full of ghosts!

The Brick Hotel may have more ghostly guests than living ones!

Our guide told us that the train stopped nearby, so many people had passed through this hotel during their travels. It was difficult to decide who to focus on first, so we just went room to room. The spirit of the woman seemed to be the strongest. She traveled throughout the hotel and gave the impression of this being her home.

I asked if the hotel had ever been a private home and was told that it was. There had been a public house there for some time prior to 1744. The property was leased to a farmer named Amos Strickland in 1748 for twenty years. He built a two-story brick building in 1763 that served as a residence, which was converted to a tavern in 1780.

Mr. Strickland is said to have played host to George Washington and his officers, and also to some captured Hessian soldiers. Perhaps the same soldiers I picked up on in the basement? Amos Strickland died in 1779 and his children sold the house. The hotel passed through many hands prior to the present owners.

We had a complete tour of the building and encountered many spirits in the various rooms and hallways. One of the most interesting spirits was that of a young man who stayed there often and called himself an actor. He was also a thief and made his living by breaking into rooms while the occupants were out and stealing their valuables. He indicated that he still enjoys going into the rooms of guests and going through their things, so if you are a guest there, remember to lock up your valuables!

Two sad spirits were small children that we encountered in one of the rooms. One was wearing a yellow nightgown and seemed to have passed away from an illness. The illness gave him a high fever and caused him to cough, so we were thinking maybe it was tuberculosis or influenza, both of which were rampant in the late 1800s and early 1900s.

So many people have passed through the Brick Hotel, it is nearly impossible to identify who these spirits may have been. The best way to describe this place is that it has a unique and striking energy, inviting and also very haunted!

TRAVELER'S NOTE

1 East Washington Avenue
Newtown, Pennsylvania 18940
www.brickhotel.com/

HOTEL CONNEAUT
PENNSYLVANIA

The Hotel Conneaut was opened in 1893 as a resort on Conneaut Lake. A carousel was added some time later and more rides were added until it became Conneaut Lake Park in 1920, to bring the focus more on the rides and amusements. Through it all, the hotel provided a convenient place to stay when visiting the park and the lake.

In 1943, the hotel was struck by lightning and the main dining room, main lobby, and approximately 150 guest rooms were destroyed in the ensuing fire. The damaged part of the hotel was demolished and not rebuilt; instead, the hotel was remodeled. The ghost stories started after the fire, which is said to have claimed the life of Elizabeth, a bride who was staying at the hotel for her honeymoon. Now it is said that Elizabeth haunts the hotel, especially the third floor.

Whoever the ghost is, staff have found lights on in rooms that are locked and unoccupied and have found windows wide open after they have checked to make sure that they were closed. One staff member even reported feeling a presence of something push between him and the wall. Was it Elizabeth?

There seems to be no record of an Elizabeth or anyone else who died in the fire; and anyway, that section of the hotel was demolished. So who haunts the hotel? No one really seems to know for sure; perhaps a very satisfied guest has decided to spend his or her afterlife there because a woman in white has been seen on the second and third floors of the hotel.

According to one visitor, Elizabeth is not the only ghost there. She encountered a ghost named John that is said to haunt the downstairs lounge. This guest reported that in spite of many attempts to take a photograph of her children in front of the fireplace, she could not get a clear photo. She turned and took some photos of other areas, which came out crystal clear. She turned back to the fireplace, and this time, her camera shut off completely. She turned it back on and quickly snapped about six photos before the kids got bored. All but one of the photos was completely blurry. When she asked the staff about it they told her that many people have difficulty taking photos in front of the fireplace and they blame that on the spirit of a man named John.

In addition to her experience with John, this guest reported two other experiences. The first was that during the night after a fireworks display just above the hotel, they were awakened by a noise that sounded like a safe being dropped from a ten-story building. Was this the spirits expressing displeasure with something that could possibly cause another fire?

The second encounter was with a ghost that she believed was the spirit of a little girl who accidentally rode her tricycle down a flight of stairs. She felt very strongly that the stairs to the basement were the stairs she died on because she could not go down those stairs. She swore it was as if a force was holding her back from going down. There are many variations of where the little girl supposedly rode her bike to her death, but the basement door is one area where it would be easy to think you were going out when really, you are going to go down very steeply.

The hotel is beautiful, but if you go please be aware that the hotel does not have an elevator, in-room television, microwaves, or refrigerators in the rooms. The best time of year to go is the spring or fall when the hotel is quieter.

TRAVELER'S NOTE

12382 Center Street
Conneaut Lake, Pennsylvania 16316
www.clphotelconneaut.com/

JEAN BONNET TAVERN
PENNSYLVANIA

When you are traveling down the Pennsylvania Turnpike, make time to stop at this historic and haunted restaurant in Bedford. The Jean Bonnet has been serving travelers since early 1762 and it is believed the tavern was built on the site of a French fort that is pictured on area maps from the 1740s. It was a prime location; first on the trade route for the Shawnee Indians, then at the intersection of two major roads. It got the name from one of its early proprietors, Jean Bonnet (pronounced the French way: "Jzon Bunnay"), who operated the tavern from 1779 to 1815.

We entered the tavern on a beautiful spring day and were seated just inside the door. Nothing appeared out of the ordinary. The restaurant had a typical rustic, colonial atmosphere. While we waited for our food, we wondered which part of the building, if any, was haunted. We walked around the dining area, soaking up the ambiance.

159

When I sat down at the table, I saw something streak by the window above us. I assumed it was a car, but made sure to keep an eye out in case it happened again.

Sure enough, it happened two more times. I couldn't wait to get outside and see if it was possible for a passing car to cause the effect I noticed.

After investigation, I could see there was no possible way for the streak to have been caused by a passing automobile. It was not really fast enough anyway, and seemed to be more the gait of a running human or a horse.

This tavern, which is built on the site of a French fort, has a long history of sadness and violence. Most of the history that we have is from the time of the English settlement. The tavern was a welcome stop along that long route to the frontier. In its early days, its status as a landmark led to it being chosen as the place to hold legal proceedings every month. In addition to the normal grievances and arguments, the tavern was also the site of what can only be described as a lynching.

Coincidentally, during one legal session, chaos broke out when a man barged into the building with a large band of Shawnee Indians on his trail. It was determined that the man had stolen a horse from the Shawnee, a crime which was, back then, punishable by hanging.

Surrounded by the Shawnee, and fearing for their own safety if they offered the man protection, the sitting judge gave the man a short hearing and passed judgment. The verdict: "Guilty!"

The man was hanged in the tavern hallway and his corpse was given to the Shawnee to prove that the theft had been avenged. It was unclear exactly which hallway the hanging occurred in, but the hallway outside the bar on the second floor was singled out by all of us as having a decidedly eerie feeling.

We felt that a ghostly woman was staring out this window.

We had stopped at the Jean Bonnet, like many travelers before us, on our way to Pittsburgh from Philadelphia. It wasn't a busy day at the tavern, but it was a beautiful one, and my three daughters enjoyed exploring the old inn and tavern. In addition to being drawn to the hallway outside the bar, we also felt the presence of a young woman looking out the window shown in the image.

One of my daughters insisted there was "something" in the attic. We stood together by the door, but could get no farther than she and I agreeing that the energy there seemed charged somehow with expectation, as if someone was waiting for us to turn the doorknob, open the door, and walk up.

I later discussed my visit to the Tavern with author and investigator Patti Wilson, who has investigated the location many times and is an expert on its history. She was intrigued by the impression I had of something passing by the window and encouraged me to look into the history of the place, especially during the time the French fort was located there, for answers. Maybe what I saw was passing travelers out of times past, traveling down the old route, far below the cars flying by above on the turnpike.

I asked her about the lady at the window and she told me a sad story of a woman who had been the mistress of a past owner. He could not marry her because he was already married with a family elsewhere. She stayed at the tavern and kept him company while he was there. She waited and pined away for him while he was away. Years passed and she remained faithful, always watching at an upstairs window for his return.

At one point, the mistress fell ill, and as it became clear that she would not recover, she sent word to her lover to come and be with her. He did not or could not, and she died there, alone and waiting, as she did in life. If our feelings were correct, she has spent her afterlife waiting as well.

When I heard that story, my heart went out to the poor woman. I wondered if anyone had made an effort to help her move on to a happier place. I don't know her name, but I know her window. Every day, when I do my meditation, I send out a little love to her.

TRAVELER'S NOTE

6048 Lincoln Highway
Bedford, Pennsylvania 15522
www.jeanbonnettavern.com/

BATTLEFIELDS AND FORTS

MONMOUTH BATTLEFIELD
NEW JERSEY

Over 100 soldiers perished the day of the battle from sunstroke. The number of victims would have been higher had it not been for the selfless acts of Mary Ludwig Hays, more commonly known as Molly Pitcher.

She was an "army wife" who followed her husband after he enlisted in the Patriot cause. It was a hot day and Mary saw that someone needed to bring water to cool the guns and also for the fallen and fatigued to drink. She brought pitcher after pitcher to the battlefield, and that is how she got her nickname. During the battle, her husband was wounded and fell. She came to him, treated his wound, and then proceeded to take over his post as a cannon rammer.

Many visitors to the park have reported being offered water by a woman in colonial clothing. When they remark on the woman at the museum they are then informed that there is no one dressed as Molly Pitcher.

Molly is not the only ghost on the battlefield. During the battle, a young wounded soldier sat against a tree in the churchyard to rest and was struck by an enemy cannonball, losing his entire arm and shoulder. He has been seen wandering the churchyard.

The church was used as a field hospital during the battle and it is said that the attending physicians waded in blood up to their ankles as they tended the fallen. The pews are still said to bear the marks of the saws from amputations performed there. It is no wonder that phantom screams and feelings of unrest are said to emanate from the church.

TRAVELER'S NOTE

Monmouth Battlefield State Park
347 Freehold Road,
Manalapan, New Jersy 07726

POINT LOOKOUT LIGHTHOUSE
MARYLAND

Since 1830, this lighthouse has stood on a narrow piece of land between the Chesapeake Bay and the mouth of the Potomac. It was a functioning lighthouse until 1966, when "the Coast Guard turned the lighthouse over to the Navy and extinguished the light."[25] In 1980, the first official paranormal investigation took place when Hans Holzer was invited there by the resident. They encountered a few spirits during their visit, including a woman with suicidal tendencies and a man who paced the hall.

Since then, residents of and visitors to the lighthouse have reported encounters with spirits, leading this lighthouse to be labeled as one of the most haunted lighthouses in America. We took advantage of the opportunity provided by the Friends of the Lighthouse to conduct a paranormal investigation one night in early spring. (This program is available to anyone who wants to go, for a nominal fee, and is currently their main fundraiser.)

One of the most haunted lighthouses in the U.S.

We were first drawn to a room on the second floor of the lighthouse. We set up our equipment and settled down for an EVP session. Right away, our sensors began going off, and Stacy, one of our group members, began to get the impression of the spirit of a small girl. I felt that she was sick and was very thirsty and wanted a cup of milk. Stacy reported feeling as if the little girl had come over and curled up in her lap.

We were gratified to find out that one of the keepers had a small daughter who was only four years old when she passed away from an illness. When we heard the story of her death, we all got a chill. She had curled up in her mother's lap and then died.

I also had a strong impression of lots of sick people around and a very bad smell coming from outside. According to our guides, right next to the lighthouse was a Civil War-era hospital. Conditions were said to be very bad as it was overcrowded and understaffed. Some people have seen the ghosts of patients on the grounds of the lighthouse. I can only imagine what the smell must have been like if conditions were as bad as all that.

I picked up on a woman in a hallway upstairs that was pacing up and down. Interestingly, as I said this, the motion detectors in the hallway began going off in order and then back down again, just as if someone were pacing. The guides told us that people have reported seeing a woman in a long, blue dress there, and some have seen a man pacing the hall. At one point, we even saw a shadow form in the hallway, which set off a motion detector and was followed by a spike on an EMF meter.

In all, it was a very eventful night and the lighthouse definitely earned its reputation as one of the most haunted in America.

TRAVELER'S NOTE

Point Lookout State Park
Scotland, Maryland
www.dnr.state.md.us/publiclands/southern/pointlookout.asp

RED BANK BATTLEFIELD
NEW JERSEY

Red Bank Battlefield was the site of a brief but decisive battle in the American Revolution. The Patriots were outnumbered three to one, but were able to successfully repel and soundly defeat the Hessian troops that advanced on them from the surrounding forest. The fort was actually located in the apple orchard of an adjacent house owned by James and Ann Whitall.

The ghosts of some of the Hessian soldiers killed that day have been seen in and around what is now a battlefield park. The trenches are still visible and the men that fell that day are still buried where they fell on the battlefield. Some were buried after they succumbed to their injuries. The Whitall house was used as a field hospital during the battle. The Whitalls were Quakers, so they tended the wounded of both sides. In the front parlor is a large stain on the floor said to be blood from one of the wounded men. There were wounded men in the house from the first floor all the way up to the attic. One soldier in particular chose to introduce himself to us during a visit to the Whitall house.

He was disturbed by the uniform on display there; he insisted it had to be a green uniform. I asked the guide about that and he agreed. Although the uniform on display is a red coat, the uniform should probably be a dark green Hessian coat.

During our visits to the house, the kitchen always seemed to be an active area. Unexplained bangs, knocks, and

A mist forming near a uniform in the Whitall House.

noises emanate from the empty kitchen as if someone is still there working. One particular day, the presence in the kitchen, which I saw as a female servant, made her presence known in a dramatic way.

There were a couple of noisy children in the house, yelling and playing some kind of tag-type game. We were relieved that they were asked to leave by the docent. We were enjoying the tour of the house and were entering the kitchen when we heard a tremendous crash. As we went down the stairs, we saw that the metal piece to the oven had not only come off the wall, but had traveled over a table and landed with a loud bang on the floor.

The guide seemed mystified by how this could have happened and he picked it up and replaced it. I felt that there was a young woman there who was very unhappy with the behavior of the children and she had thrown that piece of the oven onto the floor to make her displeasure known. "Children should be seen and not heard," was her philosophy. She seemed to be trying to go about the daily business of kitchen work and did not like to be disturbed or interrupted.

TRAVELER'S NOTE

Red Bank Battlefield Park
100 Hessian Avenue
National Park, New Jersey 08063
www.co.gloucester.nj.us/depts/p/parks/parkgolf/redbank/default.asp

FORT DELAWARE
DELAWARE

The first time I visited this Civil War fortress in the middle of a swampy area of the Delaware River, I didn't know it was supposed to be haunted. As we walked around the parade ground, the sally port, and the various tunnels and casemates, I could not shake a feeling of overwhelming sadness that seemed to cling to the place.

There is a legend about the formation of this island; that a boat carrying a load of peas tipped over and spilled the peas into the mud. They took root and grew and the island started to expand from there. The island was in existence in the late 1700s, and L'Enfant, the architect that designed Washington, D.C., suggested that a fort be built on the island since it was in a very strategic location south of Wilmington and Philadelphia. As a result of his request, a few buildings were erected there, but the fort as we see it now was completed in 1859.

A bright orb at Fort Delaware.

At the time of its completion, it was a state-of-the-art facility, capable of repelling any naval attack on the port cities. The Confederacy was not really known for its naval prowess, so Fort Delaware never saw any combat. The Union decided to use the fort in the only way it could and turned it into a prison camp.

In 1862, the first Confederate prisoners of war arrived. Shortly after this, the fort was visited by the Union Army's commissary general for prisoners. He thought the fort was a perfect place for a prison and the transfers began. Instead of taking its place in history as a bastion of Union defense, Fort Delaware is known as one of the most notorious military prisons of its time. It is often referred to as "The Andersonville of the North." Conditions were so brutal that approximately 2,300 prisoners succumbed to disease, a worse record than the Andersonville prison. According to an article by James A. Cox in the *Civil War Times* for July-August 1993:

> ...[Fort Delaware] had the highest death rate of any Union prison, and through a combination of dreadful location, official mismanagement, and political malice and vengeance, it managed to develop its own style of shocking, inhuman treatment.[26]

Unruly prisoners were kept in the casemates, which were small, dark areas originally constructed to store ammunition. In 1920, Captain F.W. Gano wrote in his History of Army Posts:

> A point of interest sought by visitors is…a dungeon in which one of the Confederate prisoners wrote his name on the wooden ceiling. The inscription reads, "Thomas Wensley, Fort Delaware, April 5, 1862."[27]

All of the so-called dungeons contained these wooden ceilings, floors, and walls, which have since rotted away. As mentioned, these casemates are small and dark. The only air and light comes from small slits in the walls. It would not take much time for a healthy man to become unhealthy in these dungeons. In fact, visitors to the fort have reported cries and moans coming from these casemates. Phantom footsteps have been heard pacing in these empty cells as well. Others have reported bright glowing lights emanating from the casemates, which disappear upon closer inspection.

One little casemate drew my attention and I felt compelled to return there and sit inside. There was a definite presence of a man there, who was dressed in ragged clothing and appeared to be in some kind of distress, pacing back and forth, trying to figure out how he was going to get out of there. He was oblivious to the fact that there was no longer a door on the casemate. Attempts at communication were unsuccessful and he seemed completely wrapped up in his own time and space.

I asked one of the guides about this area and he was visibly excited. He said he was dressed as James Archer, a Confederate officer who he believed had been held in that very casemate after plotting an escape attempt. Many prisoners attempted to escape and were caught.

The guide asked me if I had experienced anything else at the fort and I replied that there were several areas of the fort that were inhabited by spirits. One was the area above the sally port. There were a number of original bunks up there and actual cells with barred windows. This was where the Confederate officer prisoners had been held. The feeling here was of several male presences; some were guards and others were prisoners.

The guide, who was excited by our findings, then shared an experience that he had at the fort. One day, while he was making his final rounds of the fort to make sure that no visitors lingered, he noticed something moving in one of the archways. As he moved closer to investigate, he was able to make out the shadowy form of a woman, dressed in the typical hoop skirt of the 1860s. He stood, transfixed, as the shadow paced back and forth across the opening, and then disappeared. He admitted that when he is alone and has to pass that area now, he does so very quickly.

Another female spirit has been encountered in the kitchen. A group of female historic interpreters were in the kitchen with some children, preparing period foods. At one point, a woman looked up from the table where she was slicing vegetables and saw an African-American woman in a long dress and apron standing in the corner. The woman appeared to be in her thirties and had a scar on her face. The woman walked over to the pots on the stove, looked inside, and then vanished. She has been seen other times as well, always in a long dress that many remarked was burnt all around the bottom. This has led to speculation that she perished in a kitchen fire, but I do not believe so. The feeling I got was that she was very devoted to her work there and was still checking on things, making sure they were done to her satisfaction. It was not unusual for kitchen workers to have singed skirts. This was due to cooking on an open hearth. Often the bottom of the dress would smolder or even catch fire. They wore woolen fabrics because they were slow to burn, so her long, singed dress marks her as a kitchen worker, not a fire victim.

Some visitors have reported seeing the ghosts of Union soldiers, but the most common sightings are those of Confederates. A few lucky tourists have snapped photos in the fort and had ghostly Confederate soldiers show up in them. Other visitors have actually seen Confederate soldiers that they mistook for interpreters until they vanished in front of them.

During our visits to the fort, we have experienced unusual temperature fluctuations, cold spots, and unearthly voices. The temperature fluctuations and cold spots seemed to always be accompanied by camera malfunctions, making it difficult to capture anything on film.

TRAVELER'S NOTE

Delaware City, Delaware 19706
www.destateparks.com/park/fort-delaware/index.asp

THE HEADLESS HORSEMAN
OF WELSH TRACT CHURCH
DELAWARE

Welsh Tract Road and the church were part of the Battle of Cooch's Bridge on September 3, 1777. There was a group of colonists who were using the stone walls of the church as a shield against the British rifle fire. Legend has it that a young patriot named Charlie Miller was one of the Patriots. Charlie got into the line of cannon fire and the cannonball that landed in the church's wall also took his head right off. The repair work from the cannonball is still visible today.

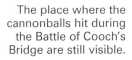
The place where the cannonballs hit during the Battle of Cooch's Bridge are still visible.

Shortly after the battle, reports started circulating that British soldiers were being attacked by a headless man on horseback, who ran them down and chopped off their heads, while calling out eerily, "I Want My Head!" Yes, I do wonder how he says anything without a head.

We went to the church on a dark and gloomy Saturday night in search of the headless horseman. I even wore my red coat in the hopes that would bring him out. I walked all around the grounds and the road in my red coat. I didn't see anything or hear anything unusual. The headless horseman was a no show. Either that or he could tell from our accents we weren't British.

TRAVELER'S NOTE

Welsh Tract Road
Newark, Delaware 19713

USS CONSTELLATION
MARYLAND

This ship museum is docked at the Inner Harbor in Baltimore. The *Constellation* began service in 1855. The ship was involved in the capture of three slave ships, protected against Rebel raids during the Civil War, and was part of a training program for U.S. Naval Officers. It's also believed to be haunted.

We had the good fortune to investigate this impressive piece of American history and found these claims to be true. The most active areas were the sick bay and the Orlop Deck. The energy in the sick bay was so heavy that it was difficult to remain in the area. As I passed the stairs from the berth deck to the lower Orlop Deck, I saw a young boy, about12 years old, staring up at me from the bottom of the steps.

He had on a dark cap, white shirt, and dark pants. As I was looking at him, he vanished. The next day, we were at Westminster Cemetery and our guide asked if anything had happened on the *Constellation*. I related my experience and she replied that the last group that had been on the *Constellation* had seen the same boy! I feel that he was one of the "powder monkeys." Powder monkeys were boys, aged 11 and up, who served in the U.S. Navy by carrying gun powder from the magazine to the gun deck when needed.

TRAVELER'S NOTE

301 E. Pratt Street
Baltimore, Maryland 21202
www.historicships.org/constellation.html

BURIED TREASURE
AND PIRATE GHOSTS

In addition to such notorious pirates like Captain Kidd, Blackbeard, and Captain Morgan, there were a number of lesser known and probably unknown pirates that roamed the oceans, bays, and inlets around the Mid-Atlantic coast. Pirates would often bury their treasure along with any witnesses to where they buried it. One or two expendable crew members would be brought along to dig the hole and when the hole was dug and the treasure placed, the leader would execute whoever had been brought along and place their bodies on top of the treasure. This happened for two reasons. One, it was thought the spirit(s) of the murdered man or men would be disturbed if the grave was dug up; and second, it eliminated witnesses to where the treasure was buried. The treasures were not buried in sand dunes or on beaches. Sand shifts and moves and anyone who has dug a hole on a beach sees how quickly it fills up with water after only a foot or so is dug. The treasures would be buried in the woods a little ways from the beach, and trees and rocks would be marked to make finding the treasure easier.

In case you think these buried treasures are just legend, know that some treasures have been recovered! Shortly after Captain Kidd was arrested, one of his treasure caches was dug up on a small island off the coast of Long Island, New York. In addition, occasionally gold coins, jewelry, and even unset gems are found washed up on beaches from New York to Virginia.

CAPE HENLOPEN
DELAWARE

Legend has it that Captain Kidd buried a chest of gold in the Cape Henlopen sand dunes during a visit in 1700 on his trip to the West Indies. Blackbeard's ghost is said to wander the shores of Black Bird Creek at Cape Henlopen, looking for a treasure that was lost when his ship sank in the creek. The ghost of Captain Kidd has not been reported, but some members of his crew have.

James Gillian, a member of Kidd's crew, buried a secret stash of gold on Kelly Island in the Delaware Bay, between two bare trees and a large rock. He was going to return and claim the treasure after Kidd was executed, but he never did. Now his spirit is said to haunt the area. Is he trying to claim the treasure or guard it from others?

Cape Henlopen State Park
Lewes, Delaware 19958
www.destateparks.com/park/cape-henlopen/park-office.asp

CAPE MAY
NEW JERSEY

Another favored site for burying treasure was Cape May, New Jersey. This spot was popular with pirates and other sailors because there was an abundant source of fresh water here at Lake Lily. Blackbeard is said to have buried some of his treasure near Higbee Beach.

Stede Bonnet is said to have buried some of his treasure there as well. Stede Bonnet was another early eighteenth-century pirate. He had been a well-to-do landowner at one time, but for some reason turned to piracy in 1717. For some time, he worked with Blackbeard, pirating ships all up and down the Eastern Coast of the U.S. It is likely that, during his time with Blackbeard, he became acquainted with Cape May. Stede's treasure is said to be buried along the Delaware Bay, north of the Cape May – Lewes Ferry terminal. "Sources indicate it was buried near the settlement of Town Bank."[28] If this is true, then it is probably underwater now, since Town Bank lost its fight with erosion and is now completely flooded.

TRAVELER'S NOTE

Higbee Beach
New England Road (on the south shore of the Delaware Canal)

TUCKER'S ISLAND
NEW JERSEY

All that remains of this once-popular resort is a shoal, but in the late 1800s, it boasted seasonal as well as year-round residents and a life-saving station. It is the life-saving station that is the source for the following treasure story.

One night the men in the station were enjoying a peaceful time when they were disturbed by the arrival of two rather rough-looking men. The men wanted to know the location of a pair of cedar trees, which were generally seen as a local landmark. The crew members pointed the way and watched the men take off in the direction of the trees. A little while later the crew spied the men dragging a large object towards their boat. Understandably concerned, the crew called for help, but the men managed to escape.

Back by the trees there was now a huge hole, an old wooden trunk, a map, some gold coins, and a rusty cutlass. It appeared that the bulk of the treasure had been made away with by the mysterious visitors.

Twenty years later, the island was beginning to erode away; and by 1930, the lighthouse and life-saving station were claimed by the ocean. The fantastic story remained, though. It would probably be dismissed except for one thing; the rusty cutlass is still on display at the Long Beach Island Historical Association.

TRAVELER'S NOTE

Long Beach Island Historical Asscoaiation
Engleside and Beach Avenues
Beach Haven, New Jersey 08008
www.lbimuseum.org/

BURLINGTON
NEW JERSEY

It was a dark and stormy night in 1717 and the men were glad to land in Burlington, New Jersey. They were pirates, sailing with the infamous Blackbeard, and had a load of treasure to bury that night.

Blackbeard decided to bury the goods under a black walnut tree on Wood Street.

He asked for a volunteer to stay and guard the treasure and when one brave soul volunteered, Blackbeard shot him dead on the spot. He buried him right there, with his pet dog, to stand guard over the treasure. Where is the treasure now? Well if you wait for another dark and stormy night, look for the ghostly man and dog. They are said to still stand guard there near the tree where it is buried.

TRAVELER'S NOTE

Wood Street
Burlington, New Jersey 08016

PLANK HOUSE
PENNSYLVANIA

My first acquaintance with this house was during a walking tour in Marcus Hook, Pennsylvania. Guides showed us a photo that the owner had taken of a ghostly man's face in the fireplace. It is an eerie photo and can be viewed at the Plank House or in Charles Adams' book *Delaware County Ghost Stories.*

I didn't have a chance to actually investigate the house until a few years later when I started volunteering with the Marcus Hook Preservation Society. I had heard all the rumors and stories and seen many published paranormal investigation reports on the web, but nothing prepared me for what I was to experience there.

I went into the house for a clean-up day and was immediately aware of the strong presence of a woman who seemed very interested in what we were doing. She followed us around all day as we cleaned windows and swept out the place. I wondered if it was the ghost of Margaret. According to Ashmead's *History of Delaware County*:

...it would be told how Blackbeard, the pirate, used to anchor his vessel off Marcus Hook, where, at the house of a Swedish woman... Margaret. He and his crew held mad revels there.[28]

175

Michael Manerchia, who used to own the house, believes the Plank House was the home of Blackbeard's mistress.

The house is an active archaeological site, and many small artifacts have been discovered, including dishes, pottery, a small cannon ball, and a fireplace with ashes still in it. It is known that renovations and digging (which are ongoing at the house) can cause spirit activity to increase. It is no wonder, then, that the presences there were so strong.

Yes, I said presences. There was more than one resident spirit at this little house. On the second floor, I encountered the spirit of a little girl. She was anxious for company and someone

A little girl haunts the second floor of the Plank House.

to talk to and play games with her. Some people have even left toys there for her.

With the woman still following us, we headed into the basement for a look around. Here we encountered a heavier and stronger presence that was definitely male. I spoke with Michael, the owner, and some of the others from the Preservation Society, and they both said they had experienced the male presence in and around the basement. Michael said that, one night, he was coming into the house and he saw a man with a large hat emerge from the basement. Since that time, he will not enter the house at night.

When we left for the day after cleaning, we noticed that the female presence that had followed us around was still with us! She followed us home and switched back and forth between myself and my associate, Beth, who had helped with the cleaning. After a couple of weeks we didn't notice her presence anymore and we wondered if she had returned to the Plank House.

We checked at our earliest convenience and found that she was back there, still watching over things. She seems to favor a corner by the front door, where there used to be a doorway that went into another room. This is now a closet right next to the dig site.

Although there is no definitive evidence that this was the house of Blackbeard's mistress, it is definitely contemporary with her. Although no pirate treasure has been found there, historical treasures have been and will continue to be unearthed at this site. Who knows? They may even stir up another ghost or two!

TRAVELER'S NOTE

221 Market Street
Marcus Hook, Pennsylvania 19061
www.marcushookps.org/MAIN-02.htm

MOUNT PLEASANT AND MACPHERSON'S GOLD
PENNSYLVANIA

Mount Pleasant was built by Captain John MacPherson, a privateer or pirate. He called the house "Clunie" after the seat of his family's clan in Scotland. This house was MacPherson's effort to join the established Philadelphia society. One thing is for sure; the house is certainly one of the most beautiful in Philadelphia and is considered one of the greatest American houses of its type.

It is thought that MacPherson hid or buried a treasure in or near his home. These would have been his takings from his years as a privateer. According to the book *Life and Times in Colonial Philadelphia* by Joseph K. Kelley, Jr., MacPherson was "the most colorful of the inhabitants...who dabbled in astronomy, complied a cryptic city directory and boasted that he invented a vermin-free bed."[29]

These few clues are all we have to go on as far as figuring out where the treasure might be.

177

BOWMAN'S HILL
PENNSYLVANIA

Said to be named after a doctor turned pirate, Dr. John Bowman, this hill in Solebury Township has been associated with buried treasure legends since the 1700s. Dr. Bowman is said to have originally set out with an English fleet whose mission it was to capture famous pirate, Captain Kidd, but Dr. Bowman changed sides and joined up with the pirate crew. After Kidd was captured, Dr. Bowman and the rest of the pirates sailed to the Delaware River, where Bowman parted company with them, traveling upriver to settle in what is now Solebury Township around 1700.

According to *The History of Bucks County* by Sallie N. Boyd, Bowman asked to be buried at the top of the hill named for him, "as that would be as near heaven as he ever expected to get." It is believed that Bowman's ghost haunts the hill, possibly to protect the treasure he is said to have buried there.

A big oak chest was listed among Dr. Bowman's possessions, but it contained no gold, fueling the rumors that he had buried the gold on the hill and requested to be buried there so he could watch over it.

Many have tried, without success to find Bowman's treasure. If you are thinking about going to look for the booty, know that digging is not allowed on Bowman's Hill. Also know that the treasure may never have been there. According to literature about Bowman's Tower from Washington Crossing Historic Park, there is no mention of a Dr. Bowman in the records of Captain Kidd's trial.

THE REFUGEES
NEW JERSEY

Joe Mulliner was the leader of a gang called the Refugees. They operated in the area of Tuckerton Road, during the American Revolution, robbing people and causing mayhem. Joe Mulliner also enjoyed dancing with pretty girls and was often seen in the local taverns, dancing and having a good time. He was always able to make his escape into the dark woods before authorities could catch up with him, until one night when his luck ran out. He was captured, tried, and sentenced to death, even though there is no record of his having murdered anyone.

He was buried on property owned by his wife and his ghost has been seen wandering the area by the Mullica River, some say to watch over the gang's ill-gotten gains, which were never recovered.

TRAVELER'S NOTE

New Jersey Pine Barrens
The grave has since disappeared.

CONCLUSION

A GHOST LAID TO REST
DELAWARE

I thought I would end this book with the story of the end of a ghost. The following is an account of how the community in Dover, Delaware solved a ghostly problem. If only they could all end happily…

The Green, at the intersection of State Street and Bank Lane was the scene of a most unusual supernatural event. It was here that the ghost of Chief Justice Samuel Chew was laid to rest in 1745. Justice Chew had passed away the year before, but he did not move on. The first sighting of the ghost of Justice Chew was by a farmer who crossed The Green on his way home late one night. He saw a shadowy form near a tree, and as he drew closer, recognized the figure as the deceased judge. A few night later, a local miller crossing the Green saw the same thing! When word got around, people were so unnerved at the thought of encountering the late judge that they began staying in after dark. The tavern keepers and business owners, feeling the pinch of reduced business, came up with an idea for "laying the ghost." A grave was dug on The Green and a funeral procession of townspeople attended a funeral service for Justice Chew, praying for the late judge to find peace. Since that day, the ghost of Chief Justice Chew was never seen again!

APPENDIX

CLEANSING

Cleansing can be done in many different ways and should be done by the property owner in order to be most effective. A common method uses sage. First, the whole area must be cleaned, as if doing a good spring cleaning. Clear out all the clutter and dust webs. Then get a sage smudge stick, available at most metaphysical supply shops, and a receptacle to safely catch the ashes in.

Open one window in each room about halfway, then light the sage stick and walk through the entire structure, allowing the smoke to flow everywhere to cleanse the area. You may even fan the smoke towards areas that seem to hold pockets of negative energy. While walking around, you should say something like:

> This sage is clearing out all negative energy and spirits. All negative energy must leave through the open windows and never return.

Continue this until the atmosphere feels lighter and more positive.

GHOST HUNTING TIPS

VISIT THE PROPERTY

Before you head out to one of the places in this book or any other place, armed with your camera, thermal scanner, EMF meter, digital recorder and more, do a preliminary check on the property during the daytime. Find out when the public is allowed access and do not trespass during hours they do not allow visitors!

ATTEMPTING CONTACT

Once you have established that you have permission to access the premises, then you may attempt to make contact with the ghosts there. All ghosts have a message to give or unfinished business they need help with. The most common messages that we receive on EVP are "hello" and "help." If a ghost is telling you to get out, it obviously wants to be left alone. Don't keep going back and bothering it. Treat the ghost as you would a living person who told you to get out.

RECORDING EVPS

How do you record EVPs? All you need is a digital recorder, a quiet place to record in, and an open mind. Then just talk aloud as if you were addressing a person in the room who you are trying to get to know. The best way to start is by introducing yourself.

PROPER ETIQUETTE

Etiquette is of the utmost importance when physically and verbally approaching a ghost. No matter who owns the property, the ghost believes that this is their territory. A ghost hunter or property owner should be respectful towards the ghost. It's important to be polite and verbally state your purpose immediately upon approaching the location. Asking the deceased individual's permission to enter the premises or to take photographs is a great way to show them they are being respected.

ANTICIPATE

Try to anticipate what the ghost may be feeling. They are usually confused, scared, and lonely. Sometimes they don't have the full understanding of where they are or what's happened to them, or they are unable to face what has happened to them. On top of that, you are a stranger with instruments pointed at them, demanding they talk to you. It is no wonder people are told to get out!

RESPECT

A disembodied human soul may be tormented by memories. They could be reliving a painful and traumatic event over and over. So be kind and respectful, and most of all, understanding.

LOOKING FOR GHOSTS?

You might want to start with a ghost tour! These tours are a great way to get started and sometimes give you access to places you wouldn't normally have access to. Please check with the tour operators to make sure you are allowed to bring cameras or any equipment you want to use.

DELAWARE

FORT DELAWARE, DELAWARE CITY, AND DELAWARE
www.mystandlace.com/events.shtml
410-398-5013

NEW CASTLE
www.newcastlehistory.org/events.html#oct
302-322-2794

ROCKWOOD MANSION
www2.nccde.org/rockwood/EventCalendar/default.aspx
302-761-4340

MARYLAND

ANNAPOLIS
www.ghostsofannapolis.com/
1-800-979-3370

BALTIMORE
www.fellspointghost.com

ELLICOTT CITY
www.howardcountymd.gov/HCT/HCT_GhostTours.htm
1-800-288-8747

FREDERICK
www.marylandghosttours.com/
301-668-8922

HAVRE DE GRACE
www.mainstreetdg.com/ArtsandEntertainment/
HauntedHistoryGhostTours.aspx
410-939-1811

NEW JERSEY

CAPE MAY
www.elainesdinnertheater.com/ghost.html
609-884-1199

KEYPORT
www.jerseyshoreghosttours.com/keyporttours.htm
732-500-6262

OCEAN CITY
www.ghosttour.com/oceancity.html
609-814-0199

PRINCETON
www.princetontourcompany.com/polGhostTours.cfm
609-902-3637

RED BANK
www.jerseyshoreghosttours.com/redbanktours.htm
732-500-6262.

PENNSYLVANIA

BETHLEHEM
www.moravianbookshop.com/more_info.aspx?ID=1480
610-866-5481

ERIE
www.eerieerie.com/
814-431-8601

GETTYSBURG
www.gettysburgbattlefieldtours.com/ghostly-images.php
717-334-629

GETTYSBURG
www.ghostsofgettysburg.com
717-337-0445

GRAEME PARK, HORSHAM
www.graemepark.org/
215-343-0965

JIM THORPE
www.jimthorperotary.org/ghostwalks.cfm
570-325-2346

LANCASTER
www.ghosttour.com/lancaster.html
717-687-6687

NEW HOPE
www.ghosttoursofnewhope.com/
215-343-5564

PHILADELPHIA
www.ghosttour.com/philadelphia.html
215.413.1997

PITTSBURGH
www.hauntedpittsburghtours.com/
412-302-5223

READING
www.exeterhousebooks.com/cgibin/buildpage.pl?main=schedule.
php&index=boo_links
610-775-0464

SCRANTON
http://scrantonghosttours.com/
570-383-1821

STRASBURG
www.ghosttour.net/strasburg.html
717-687-6687

VIRGINIA

ABINGDON
www.appalachianghostwalks.com/ghosttours/abingdonghosttour.
html
423-743-WALK

ALEXANDRIA
www.alexcolonialtours.com/graveyard.html
703-519-1749

FREDERICKSBURG
www.ghostsoffredericksburg.com/
540-710-3002

LEESBURG
www.vsra.net
571-242-6824

LEXINGTON
www.lexingtonvirginia.com/attractionsb.asp?id=22
540-464-2250

RICHMOND
www.hauntsofrichmond.com/
804-343-3700

SHIRLEY PLANTATION
www.shirleyplantation.com/aunt_pratt.html
1-800-232-1613

VIRGINIA BEACH
www.historiesandhaunts.com/ghost_walks.php
757-498-2127

WILLIAMSBURG
www.williamsburgprivatetours.com/ghost.htm
757-229-1000

WILLIAMSBURG
www.theghosttour.com/
877-62-GHOST

WASHINGTON, D.C.

Washington, D.C. Ghost Tours
www.dcghosttours.com/
888-844-3999

ENDNOTES

1. Frazer, J.G, translator. *Pausanias's Description of Greece*. 6 vols., London: Macmillan, 1913 VII, 24. 4
2. The New Jersey Bigfoot Reporting Center. www.njbigfoot.org
3. www.louisianabooknews.com/images/HauntedTravelsTimes. Oct22,2008.pdf
4. Briggs, Katherine M. (1976). *A Dictionary of Fairies.* Harmondsworth, Middlesex: Penguin. p. 52
5. Cowan, Frank. *Southwestern Pennsylvania in Song and Story*. Nabu Press, 2010. pp. 201-202
6. Kriebel, David W. *Powwowwing: A Persistent American Esoteric Tradition*. www. esoteric.msu.edu/VolumeIV/Powwow.htm
7. "Witchcraft, a part of Maryland's past." *Washington Times* 10 October 2004. www. washingtontimes.com/news/2004/oct/10/20041010-102416-3747r/
8. Semmens, Raphael. *Crime and Punishment in Early Maryland*. John Hopkins University Press, 1996. pp. 167 – 73
9. Ibid
10. Ibid
11. Hugg, David S. "The Ghosts of Southern Delaware." *Delaware Today*. October 1979
12. The Theosophical Society website. www.theosophical.org/
13. www.ushistory.org/tour/bishop-white.htm
14. www.ushistory.org/tour/washington-square.htm
15. www.ushistory.org/tour/tomb-of-the-unknown-soldier.htm
16. Watson, John F. Watson's *Annalls of Philadelphia and Pennsylvania.* 1857. www. usgwarchives.org/pa/philadelphia/watsontoc.htm
17. Ibid
18. Carpenter's Hall. Museum of the Macabre, www.museumofthemacabre.com
19. Ibid
20. "Woman Struck by Trolley Car." *Chester Times.* December 18, 1915. www3. gendisasters.com/pennsylvania/13609/drexel-hill-pa-trolley-car-accident-dec-1915
21. "The Forgotten Dead: Neglected Graves at the Old Quarantine Station at Essington." *Chester Times*, December 5, 1899
22. Brigadier General John Lacey, Jr., to General Armstrong, dated May 11, 1778
23. The Walnut Street Theatre. www.walnutstreettheatre.org/
24. National Park Service; Mount Washington Page. www.nps.gov/archive/fone/mwt.htm
25. Point Lookout website. www.ptlookoutlighthouse.com/timeline.shtml
26. Cox, James A. *Civil War Times*, July-August 1993
27. Gano, Captain F.W. *History of Army Posts*. 1920
28. Jersey Shore Pirates website. www.jerseyshorepirates.com
29. Kelley, Joseph K., Jr. *Life and Times in Colonial Philadelphia*. Stackpole Books, 1973

ADDITIONAL RESOURCES
(Listed in book order.)

Indian Echo Caverns:
Hauck, D.W. *Haunted Places: The National Directory*. Penguin, 2002.

Oley Hills Rocks:
Muller, Norman. "Accenting the Landscape: Interpreting the Oley Hills Site" by http://
rock-piles.com/oleyhill.pdf

Lost Valley Rocks
Browne, Karla. "Public gets first glimpse of local rock collection." *The Sentinal*. www.
cumberlink.com/news/article_0bd3ec24-0fe5-5879-8d90-70b1097102ab.html
Miller, Matt. "Scientists dispute significance of Lost Valley artifacts." *Penn View*,
December 15, 2004

Shrine of St. Katherine Drexel
www.vatican.va/news_services/liturgy/saints/ns_lit_doc_20001001_katharine-
drexel_en.html

Raystown Ray
Walls, Kathleen. "Raystown Royalty". www.americanroads.net/raystownlakeA.htm

Bigfoot
Dickinson, Nathan. "Tall, Elusive Creature with Big Feet Baffles Authorities." *The
Capital*. Annapolis, MD. August 1, 2000

Thunderbird
Clark, Jerome. *Unexplained!* Visible Ink Press, 1998
Lyman, Robert. *Forbidden Land. Strange Events in the Black Forest*. Volume 1 &
Volume 2. Leader Publishing Company, 1971

Goatman
____*Encyclopedia of Cryptozoology: A Global Guide*. McFarland & Company, Inc.
pp. 176
"Residents Fear Goatman Lives: Dog Found Decapitated in Old Bowie." *Prince
George's County News*. November 10, 1971

Horned Skulls
Lyman, Robert. *Forbidden Land.* Leader Publishing. Coudersport, Pennsylvania. 1971

How to Become a Witch
Vance Randolph, *Ozark Magic and Folklore.* Dover Publications, 1964. PP. 266-67

Witch's Tree
Graves, R. *Greek Myths*. Penguin, London, 1955

Margaret Mattson
Ashmead, Henry Graham. *History of Delaware County, Pennsylvania.* L.H. Everts & Co. Philadelphia, 1884. www.delcohistory.org/ashmead/index.htm
Spence, Lewis. *Encyclopaedia of Occultism*. University Press, New Hyde Park, New York. 1960. pp. 347 – 349

Seth Levis
Zook. Mary. "Witch's Tale of A Levis Home and Marple Township's Pancoast House." *Upper Darby News*, December 30, 1947. Page 9

Moll De Grow
Hine, C.G. Woodside. Hine's Annual, 1909

Moll Dyer
Parke, Frances Neal. "Witchcraft in Maryland," *Maryland Historical Magazine* 31:4 (December 1936) p. 271-298.)

Delaware Witches
Craig, Dr. Peter S. *Swedish Colonial News*, Volume 2, Number 5. 2001

The First Witch
Davis, Richard Beale. "The Devil in Virginia in the Seventeenth Century." *Virginia Magazine of History and Biography*. 65 (1957) 131-49

Cursed Mine
Lankford, Andrea. *Haunted Hikes.* Santa Monica Press, 2006

Indian Curse Road
Fuhrmann, Doug. "Local history: Route 55." *The Daily Journal*. www.thedailyjournal.com/article/20090301/NEWS01/90404015. March 1, 2009

Bishop White House
"The Diseased City." http://xroads.virginia.edu/~ma96/forrest/ww/fever.html

Lafayette Square
www.nps.gov/nr/travel/wash/dc30.htm

Decatur House
www.decaturhouse.org/

Hay Adams Hotel
www.hayadams.com/

Fiddler's Bridge
Federal Writer's Project. *Delaware: A Guide to the First State.* Reprint Services Corp,1938

Baleroy
Lear, Len. "Visitors didn't stand a 'ghost of a chance.' George G. Meade Easby, a one-of-a-kind Hiller." *Chestnut Hill Local,* December 15, 2005

Lazaretto
Ashmead, Henry Graham. *History of Delaware County, Pennsylvania.* L.H. Everts & Co. Philadelphia, 1884. www.delcohistory.org/ashmead/index.htm

Rockwood Mansion
"History of the Bringhurst Family." www.archive.org/stream/historyofbringhu00leac/historyofbringhu00leac_djvu.txt
Silverman, Sharon Hernes. *Brandywine Valley: The Informed Traveler's Guide.* Mechanicsburg: Stackpole Books, 2004. pp. 188-194

Grumblethorpe
Fink, Rick. "Ghosts of the Great Road: Do Bloodstains Mark Spot of a Ghostly Presence?" *Germantown Chronicle*, October 22, 2009

The Massey House
Butler, Mary. "Two Lenape Rock Shelters near Philadelphia." Society for American Archaeology,1947

Bloomsburg University
Gabel, Erin. "Six Roommates Gain A Ghostly Seventh." *The Voice.* October 30, 2003

Hopkins, Amanda. "Sorority haunted by entity." *The Voice*. October 14, 2009

Piz, Mia and Seda, Jessica. "Investigating Campus and Town Ghost Stories." *The Voice.* October 23, 2001

Zarko, Michelle. DFE "Sisters Haunted By Eerie Spirits." *The Voice.* October 30, 2003

The George School
www.georgeschool.org

McGinnis, James. "Faculty Tell GS Ghost Stories." *Bucks County Courier Times*, October 21, 2010

Hotel Conneaut
www.clphotelconneaut.com/index.html

Smith, Ryan. "Staff have ghostly experiences at Hotel Conneaut." *The Meadville Tribune*. October 20, 2006

The Jersey Devil
McCloy, James and Miller, Ray. *Phantom of the Pines: More Tales of the Jersey Devil*. Middle Atlantic Press, 1998. New Jersey Devil Hunters. www.njdevilhunters.com

Tucker's Island
New Jersey History's Mysteries Website. www.njhm.com/

Burlington, New Jersey
Sarapin, Janice Kohl. *Old Burial Grounds of New Jersey: A Guide.* Rutgers University Press, 2002

Plank House
Ashmead, Henry Graham. *History of Delaware County, Pennsylvania.* L.H. Everts & Co. Philadelphia, 1884. www.delcohistory.org/ashmead/index.htm

INDEX